The Cambridge Manuals of Science and
Literature

THE THEORY OF MONEY

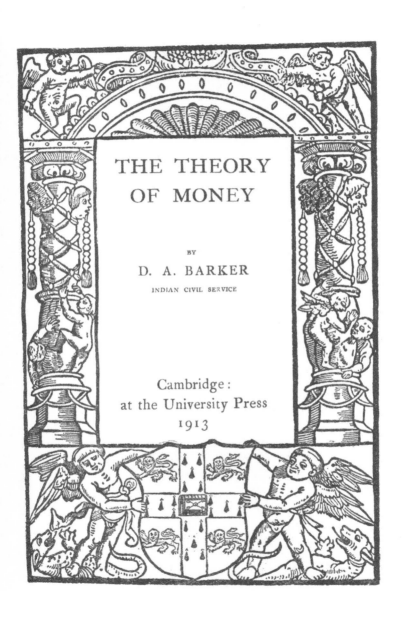

THE THEORY OF MONEY

BY

D. A. BARKER

INDIAN CIVIL SERVICE

Cambridge:
at the University Press
1913

CAMBRIDGE UNIVERSITY PRESS
Cambridge, New York, Melbourne, Madrid, Cape Town,
Singapore, São Paulo, Delhi, Tokyo, Mexico City

Cambridge University Press
The Edinburgh Building, Cambridge CB2 8RU, UK

Published in the United States of America by Cambridge University Press, New York

www.cambridge.org
Information on this title: www.cambridge.org/9781107659933

© Cambridge University Press 1913

First published 1913
First paperback edition 2011

A catalogue record for this publication is available from the British Library

ISBN 978-1-107-65993-3 Paperback

*With the exception of the coat of arms at
the foot, the design on the title page is a
reproduction of one used by the earliest known
Cambridge printer, John Siberch, 1521*

PREFACE

IT has been well said that in England of recent years the theory of money has become a matter of oral tradition. In the United States, on the other hand, there has been, during the last fifteen years, a flood of literature which contains works of the highest interest and importance, and which has carried the theory of money definitely beyond the point at which it was left by Jevons. To the English student, of course, this literature is easily available, and he cannot do better than study the originals. These originals, however, are often so bulky or so technical as to discourage the general reader, and I have therefore attempted in this book to set forth the more important results of recent American work, without omitting those divisions of the subject which are better known to English students. Taken together with *Cash and Credit*, already published in this series, which relates chiefly to the subjects of foreign exchanges and banking, I hope that this book will give the reader a fairly thorough acquaintance with the theory of money, and will encourage him to turn to original sources. To these sources, especially to American authors such as Messrs

Laughlin, Kemmerer, and Irving Fisher, I have to acknowledge a very large debt. Indeed the portion of this book dealing with " velocity of circulation " is practically a *précis* of the corresponding chapters of Professor Irving Fisher's book, *The Purchasing Power of Money*. To the perusal of this work, as well as of Professor Kemmerer's *Money, Credit and Prices*, I would commend every reader. Professor Jevon's *Money* is almost too well known to need a reference. In conclusion, I would advise the more advanced student to study the evidence of Dr Alfred Marshall given before the Gold and Silver Commission, and also the monetary chapters of Professor Sidgwick's *Principles*.

LANSDOWNE, GARHWAL,
   March 1913.

CONTENTS

THE THEORY OF MONEY

CHAPTER I

MONEY : THE MEDIUM OF EXCHANGE

MONEY is the medium of exchange, and where there is no exchange there will be no need for money. If we can imagine a community of which every member provided for himself, built his own house, made his own clothes, found and cooked his own food, and sought out his own amusements, we shall see that in such a community money would be a useless commodity, just as useless, indeed, as it would be to a Robinson Crusoe. Each being sufficient to himself would have no use for the productions or the accomplishments of others, and would set no value upon them. With no wish to purchase there would be no need for money, and money, therefore, would not exist. But, man being a social animal, we cannot expect to find societies of self-sufficing individuals such as we have imagined. We do find, however, in forms more or less perfect, self-sufficing *communities* the members of which use little or no money. Such communities have

A

practically no external trade, as their members find in each other's activities satisfaction for all of the small number of wants which they possess.   Within the community the use of money is avoided by the simple but clumsy method of barter.   Even at the present day we may find, in India or in Russia, villages having practically no connection with the outside world, and of which the members, living on the produce of their own fields, make each a yearly contribution in kind towards the support of a village priest, a potter, a carpenter or a scavenger, who supplies his services in return.   Such moneyless societies, however, are rapidly disappearing amidst the stress of competition encountered from without, though in the sheltered study of the communist philosopher they continue to arise in more ambitious and more stable forms.

In the present constitution of society, however, it would seem that the adoption of a " money " is essential to industrial progress.   The most productive methods and the most skilled workmen can only be employed in response to a very large demand ; and a large demand implies considerable division of labour.   Were everyone to make his own loaves and his own beer, instead of entrusting that work to bakers and to brewers, the average excellence of both bread and beer would certainly be lowered ; but, as man cannot live by bread alone and still less by beer, the very existence of bakers and of brewers, devoting their whole time to the production of one commodity, depends upon their being able to exchange the greater part of this one commodity for the products of others. The division of labour, in short, depends upon exchange of products, and everything which facilitates exchange will facilitate division of labour. It is as an aid to exchange, and hence to the division of labour, that the invention of money has proved of such vast importance to mankind.

It will be instructive to notice some of the difficulties to which the business of exchange is subject in the absence of a monetary economy, and from which it will be freed by the adoption of a " money." Without money exchange can only be carried on by means of barter, and barter is subject to many inconveniences. In the first place there is the difficulty of bringing about a *coincidence of wants*. Thus, if a man wishes to buy a pair of boots, and has a coat to give in exchange, he will have to find not merely a man who wishes to part with a pair of boots, but a man who wishes to part with a pair of boots in exchange for a coat, and such a person may not be immediately discoverable. When Dr Wallace was travelling in the islands of the Malay Archipelago, where no proper currency existed, he sometimes found great difficulty in getting food because the

men who had the food did not want any of the
articles which Dr Wallace possessed. He therefore
took to carrying about with him knives, cloth, sago-
cakes, and other miscellaneous articles with which
to tempt the varying tastes of the native traders.
Another instance of this difficulty, quoted by the
late Professor Jevons in his *Money*, is that of a
singer from the *Théâtre Lyrique*, who, in the course of
a professional tour round the world, gave a concert
in the Society Islands. Her remuneration was a
share of the receipts, and eventually materialized in
three pigs, twenty-three turkeys, forty-four chickens,
five thousand cocoanuts, and considerable quantities of other fruits. Here there was certainly no
coincidence of wants. The Society Islanders, no
doubt, wanted to hear Mlle. Zélie sing, but Mlle.
Zélie certainly did not want five thousand cocoanuts.

What is obviously needed in such a case is the
existence of a commodity which would be equally
acceptable to all persons, or, at any rate, to all persons
inhabiting a particular neighbourhood, and which,
therefore, would be taken about by all who wish to
trade in that neighbourhood. Such a commodity,
as we shall see, need not necessarily be a metal,
neither need it be something which is desired, as
gold is by us, almost solely for purposes of exchange.
A commodity has often been adopted as the medium

of exchange because it is the principal product of the community — such as cattle in case of pastoral tribes, tobacco in tobacco-producing countries, and so on. By virtue of the existence of such a *medium of exchange* those who wish to buy and those who wish to sell are enabled to make their needs coincide. Everyone who wishes to buy will couch his offer in terms of the one recognized commodity which is acceptable to all. Everyone who wishes to sell will be prepared to sell in exchange for that commodity which, by reason of its general acceptability, is immediately available for further exchanges. Had such a medium of exchange existed in Melanesia, Dr Wallace would not have been obliged to buy, at the cost of painful experience, the knowledge of what particular articles were most acceptable to the Malays. He would have provided himself with *the* article of general acceptability—the " money " of Melanesia—and, armed with this, could have gone forth upon his travels freed from the anxiety that somewhere he might find a jaded savage to whom knives or sago-cakes did not appeal. The case of Mlle. Zélie is somewhat different. Here, of course, it might well have been that what was " money " in the Society Islands was not " money " in France. For the purposes of trade between different countries it is a great convenience, though not a necessity, to have an international " money "—a commodity such as gold bullion—which is freely acceptable all the world over.

A further difficulty of exchange in the absence of money is due to the necessity, under such circumstances, of fixing the terms of each bargain separately. Where bread is exchanged directly for beer, beer for hats, hats for shoes, shoes for pipes, and so on, a general price-list would be almost impossible. Such a list would require every article to be expressed in terms of every other article. A pair of shoes, for instance, might be entered as equivalent to sixty loaves of bread, to one hundred and twenty pints of beer, to six pipes, to two top-hats, and so on, *ad infinitum*. The man who asked for a top-hat might be told the price in terms of any of these equivalents, and might be quite unable to tell whether that price was extortionate or otherwise. There would be, in fact, no *common measure of value*. All buying and selling would be immensely complicated. Immediate relief, however, would be obtained by the general adoption of one commodity in terms of which all prices were to be expressed. If, for instance, corn were taken as that commodity, corn would become the common measure of value. A man wishing to buy a top-hat would then be told the price thereof in terms of corn, and, having been accustomed to buy and sell in terms of corn, would know at once whether that price was a fair one.

It is generally the case that when a commodity has been adopted as the medium of exchange it has also been adopted as the common measure of value. The reason is obvious, for where it is the custom to pay for all purchases in, say, tobacco, it is obviously convenient to express the price of such purchases in tobacco also. If, for instance, the medium of exchange were tobacco, whilst the common measure of value were corn, a man buying a hat priced at a bushel of corn would have to find out the equivalent of so much corn, as expressed in tobacco, before he knew how much tobacco to give for the hat. This identification of the medium of exchange with the measure of value is, however, by no means essential, and instances of its absence are fairly common. A homely example may still be found in the Island of Guernsey, where prices are expressed in francs but the coins commonly in circulation are English silver. The medium of exchange, that is to say, is the shilling, whilst the common measure of value is the franc.

So far we have dealt with those functions of money which facilitate exchange, and which thus have an enormous importance in giving free play to the division of labour and consequent development of trade. We have still to deal with another important, but less essential, function of money, *i.e.* the function of acting as the *standard of value*, or as it has been better termed, the *standard of deferred payments*. As the common measure of value, money is used to compare the relative values of "present" goods ; as the standard of deferred payments it is used to compare the relative value of "present" goods with that of "future" goods. The most important example of this latter use is found in the case of loans. If, for instance, a man borrow a ton of coal on an agreement to pay back two tons of coal at the end of twenty years, he may be said to take coal as his standard of deferred payments. If, at the time he borrowed, coal was scarce and valuable, whilst at the time fixed for repayment it happened to be plentiful and of little value—in other words, if there is a "depreciation of the standard "—it is obvious that the borrower will benefit and the lender will lose. If, on the other hand, the standard *appreciates* between the date of borrowing and the date of repayment it is the lender who will benefit and the borrower who will lose. Such uncertainties, due to variations in the standard, are naturally bad for trade, and it is important to adopt as the standard of deferred payments a commodity which shall be as stable as possible. Owing to the fact that the money commodity, used as the medium of exchange, has almost necessarily been adopted as the common measure of value for present goods, so it has been adopted also as the common measure of value for future goods—that is, as the standard of deferred payments. As it so happens, the money commodity of modern commerce is a fairly stable one as regards its value ; but, apart from the obvious convenience of using the same common measure of value for future as for present goods, there is no reason for using the *money* commodity, or, indeed, any other *single* commodity, as the standard of deferred payments. Thus, during the sixteenth century, when silver was the common measure of value, *corn* was required by statute to be the standard of deferred payments in drawing the leases of certain college lands. That is to say, whilst prices of present goods were expressed in shillings, engagements on account of the future rents of these college lands were expressed in bushels of corn. It could also be arranged that the standard of deferred payments should be a composite standard. The unit might consist, for instance, of a pound of iron combined with a bushel of wheat, an ounce of tea and a pound of cotton. But this extension will be referred to subsequently at greater length.

In addition to the three functions of a medium of exchange, a common measure of value and a standard of deferred payments, a fourth function—that of acting as a *store of wealth*—has been attributed to the " money " commodity. By this is meant that " money " may be used (1) to accumulate in anticipation of extraordinary expenses, and (2) to transmit wealth from place to place. But so far as the first purpose is concerned it would seem rather an occasional and accidental use of the money commodity, rather than a use of that commodity *qua* money. In some cases, of course, the principal form of wealth is used as money, as were cattle by some pastoral tribes, and in such cases any accumulation of " money " is necessarily identical with an accumulation of wealth. As regards the second purpose also, it may be sufficient to point out that export is a non-monetary use of the money commodity.

CHAPTER II

THE EVOLUTION OF MONEY

In the early history of mankind the acts implied in the word " exchange "—acts which now form the most important activity of the human race—were of comparatively rare occurrence. It would not be far from true to say that society was then composed of self-sufficing individuals grouped in self-sufficing communities. Within such a community the factors of contiguity and obvious convenience would soon call into play the device of barter ; but without the community the development did not proceed so quickly. Inter-tribal trade often begins as an interchange of presents rather than as a purely business enterprise. "It is instructive to see trade in its lowest form among such tribes as the Australians. The tough greenstone, valuable for making hatchets, is carried hundreds of miles by natives who receive from other tribes in return the prize products of their districts, such as red ochre to paint their bodies with. When strangers visit a tribe they are received at a friendly gathering or corroboree, and presents are given on both sides. No doubt there is a general sense that the gifts are to be fair exchanges, and if

11

either side is not satisfied there will be grumbling and fighting ; but in this roughest kind of barter we do not yet find that clear notion of a unit of value which is the great step in trading." And this is only natural, for the conception of a unit of value must, in general, be subsequent to the adoption of a medium of exchange, and the adoption of an inter-tribal medium of exchange must always be a slow process. An *intra*-tribal money, on the other hand, seems to be a fairly early development. As a general rule the commodity which becomes the medium of exchange is that which is the commonest form of wealth in the tribe. One reason for this would seem to be that a tribe having little or no connection with other tribes cannot afford to produce large quantities of any forms of wealth other than those which are useful to almost every member of that tribe. Now a commodity which is useful to every member of a tribe fulfils the primary con-dition of a " money," and is naturally adopted as such when the need for a money arises. Thus it is that skins are found to be used as money in hunting communities, cattle in pastoral, and corn, or other grains, in agricultural communities. In other cases a commodity may be universally desired for purposes of display, and, being universally desired, may come to be used as money. Such commodities will usually be of small bulk, and will therefore be even

better adapted for currency purposes than are the
more useful products of the tribe, *e.g.* corn or cattle.
Among the Indians of British Columbia, for example,
strings of haiqua shells are used both as ornaments
and as a medium of exchange, whilst in British India
cowrie shells, though no longer used as ornaments, are
still current in the bazaars for very small payments,
about two hundred being given for a penny.   And
it is practically certain that the precious metals, also,
have come into use as money only because they were
first used as ornaments.   Thus among savage tribes
gold and silver are used almost exclusively for
display.   In India we may see the transition stage,
where these metals are just as important for ornamental as for currency use.   In Europe and North
America we find the stage where the currency use
has become infinitely the more important of the
two.

So far we have been considering the evolution of
money in an isolated tribe.   With the development
of outside trade, however, it becomes possible for the
community to specialize in the production of important staples to be used more or less exclusively for
export.   Now a commodity for which there is always
a steady demand from without will naturally have a
fairly stable value within the community.   Persons
who possess stocks of that commodity will always be
able to export it in exchange for outside productions,

or to sell it to others who will so export it. A commodity which is thus always available for exchange will be readily taken in exchange, and so will easily develop into a " money." Thus it was that tobacco was adopted for currency purposes in Virginia, tin in the Malay Peninsula, and dried cod-fish in Newfoundland.

It will be convenient at this point to describe a most important monetary truth which is aptly illustrated by the example of primitive currencies. This is the so-called *Gresham's law*—that bad money drives out good money. Let us take the case of a currency of dried cod, and let us suppose A, an inhabitant of Newfoundland, to have in his possession a number of pieces of cod of the standard size. These A can use indifferently, either to eat or to exchange for other articles. It is obvious, then, that A will keep the freshest and most attractive pieces to eat, whilst the remainder he will use for purposes of exchange. But since everybody else will be doing the same thing—using the best pieces for consumption and passing on the worse—the cod currency will always tend to deteriorate, and will actually deteriorate, unless always kept up to the proper level by new additions. Similarly a gold currency can be used for two purposes, exchange and export, in which latter use is included melting for the arts. For export or melting weight is of the first importance, whilst for exchange, so long as the coin is not so light as to be obviously unacceptable, weight is of no importance at all. Hence the full-weight coins will be continually withdrawn for melting or export, whilst the light coins remain in circulation, and a gold currency will thus constantly tend to deteriorate just as will a cod currency.

To the political economist the natural history of money, however interesting, is not a fruitful study, and I propose, therefore, to pass on to the stage where the metals, in one form or another, have become the sole medium of exchange. The reasons on account of which the precious metals have attained to this place are fairly obvious. " Metals can not only be kept with as little loss as any other commodity, scarce anything being less perishable than they are, but they can likewise, without any loss, be divided into any number of parts, as by fusion those parts can easily be reunited again." [1] In addition to these qualities the metals are portable and can, by the aid of machinery, be put into shapes which it is difficult for the forger to imitate. Some of the metals, such as silver, gold and copper, are so coloured as to be readily distinguished from one another, and, finally, the conditions of production are generally such as to render improbable any violent fluctuations in value. All these qualities are

[1] *Wealth of Nations*, Bk. I. c. 4.

useful, if not essential, to a good medium of exchange, and it is not surprising therefore that the precious metals have succeeded in ousting all other competitors from this function.

The primitive forms of money, though marking one of the most important inventions ever devised by man, were yet inconvenient in many respects. Mere lumps of merchandise, whether these consist of dried cod-fish, of tobacco, or of silver, are of problematical quality and weight; and the man to whom a nugget of silver was tendered in payment might easily have been mistaken as to its purity if not as to its weight. It was therefore very necessary that the circulating medium should be of a uniform and known quality. When metals were adopted as the money substance, it was natural that a certain degree of fineness or purity should be recognized as the standard, and that this standard of purity should be attested by means of a stamp impressed upon the pieces of metal used as money. At first the ruler of the country simply had his seal stamped upon blocks of metal, which had been found to be of the requisite fineness, without attempting to standardize the *weight* of the blocks as well. Thus the person to whom such blocks of metal were given in payment had to weigh them in order to discover their true value. In all cases, where metals have been adopted as money, this *currency by weight, i.e.* a currency of which the units are certified as to their quality only, has been preliminary to the introduction of a *currency by tale, i.e.* a currency of which the units are certified as to their weight as well as to their quality.

The next step taken by the State towards the development of money was to impart to it the quality of *legal tender*. A particular kind of money is said to be legal tender when it is pronounced by law to be, in the absence of special contract, the proper medium wherewith to make payments or to satisfy debts. " Whatever that something is which the debtor can *compel* his creditor to receive in payment of a debt is termed . . . legal tender." [1] At this point it should be noted that a coin may be legal tender for all payments however large, or it may be legal tender for those payments only which are less than a given amount.

Where in any country a single kind of coin—for example, gold coin only—is pronounced by law to be legal tender, there is said to be a system of *single legal tender*. This system has the advantage of simplicity, but it has also this obvious disadvantage that the metal adopted will either be too valuable to be conveniently used in small transactions, or too cumbersome for large transactions. At one time silver used to be the sole legal tender in England, and in Sweden, copper. " To pay a few hundred

[1] *Theory and Practi   of Banking*, by H. D. Macleod, vol. i. p. 45.

B

pounds in Swedish copper plates . . . a cart would be required for conveyance. . . . A silver coinage again does not admit of coins sufficiently small for minor transactions." [1]   Experience shows that the inconvenience of a system of single legal tender leads to the introduction of coins of other metals, which, however bad, will generally circulate to some extent. Thus in the seventeenth century in England the absence of small change led to the issue by petty tradesmen of metal discs, which, in the absence of any other medium for small payments, came to circulate as money, sometimes over the whole of a town, sometimes only within the confines of a single street.   A more modern example of this tendency was seen a few years ago when the London County Council, during a temporary scarcity of copper coins, made an issue of metal discs for use as small change on their tramways. These tokens were refused by the public.   In South America, however, similar issues of gutta-percha tokens, made by street car companies, were accepted.

Such unregulated issues, though at first supplying a want, tend finally to become so debased as to be almost useless.   Consider, for instance, the case of a publican who finds his trade inconvenienced by the fact that his customers cannot get coins of a value sufficiently small for their purchases.   He might

[1] Jevon's *Money*, p. 97.

manufacture, say, copper discs corresponding in nominal value to a convenient fraction, say, one-twelfth, of the legal tender unit, and might persuade his clients to accept these discs in change for their large legal-tender coins. If the publican promised to take back in payment for beer all such discs tendered by his customers, a regular *habitué* of the public-house would then have no hesitation in accepting the discs in change, for he could always get rid of them in exchange for beer. If it were the custom for clients to use their discs solely in purchasing beer, it is obvious that the number of such discs issued could not be large. It would be rigidly limited by the number of customers. If, however, the convenience of the discs caused them to be accepted by shopkeepers other than the publican who issued them, the extent of the issue might be largely increased. They might first be used in the immediate neighbourhood of the public-house of issue, and finally, perhaps, throughout the whole town.

Suppose now that these copper discs are of the nominal value of one penny. Then it is obvious that the publican will not put one pennyworth of copper into each disc, for by so doing he would be a loser to the amount of the cost of coinage. He will rather deduct from each coin at least so much metal as will make up for this cost, and, in all probability, he will deduct a great deal more. When he finds

that the customers who come to his house are willing
to receive in change the coins which he presses
upon them, his desire for gain will tempt him to
manufacture these coins of cheaper metal or of
smaller size, whilst still keeping their nominal value
at one penny. Thus the quality of his issues tends
ever to deteriorate, and their quantity to increase.
It is important to determine to what extent this
process of expansion and degradation can proceed.

First, it should be noted that the copper discs
issued by our publican can be used for two purposes
only. They may be used generally as small change
throughout the town, or, specially, for buying beer
from the house of issue. They cannot be melted
down and used in the arts since, *ex hypothesi*, their
metallic value is less than the nominal value at
which they are current. They are, in fact, *token
money* as distinguished from *standard money*, of
which the value in exchange depends upon the value
of the metal contained therein. Now obviously
the two uses specified—the use as small change
within the town, and the use for purchasing beer—are
strictly limited. The first use will be limited by the
amount of trade done ; for it may be assumed that
the tradespeople of the town, other than the publican,
will expect to receive legal-tender coin when possible,
and will therefore refuse to receive more than eleven
of the discs in any one payment. The second use

will be limited by the quantity of beer consumed, if
we may omit for the moment any reference to the
velocity of circulation of the token coins. Now,
supposing that our publican, egged on by his desire
to make an easy profit through issuing over-valued
discs, continues to pass out such discs after the
legitimate demand for the two uses specified above
has been satisfied. This he will probably be able
to do before the users of the discs realize what is
happening. Sooner or later, however, someone,
probably a retail tradesman, will wake up to find
himself possessed of such a number of these discs
that he is unable to get rid of them either in purchasing beer or by passing them on to others as small
change. He will therefore refuse to receive any
more discs which may be offered him by others. The
news of this refusal will cause other persons too,
particularly tradespeople, to be chary about taking
the discs, if not to refuse them altogether. Those
persons who are so unfortunate as to be caught
with large quantities of the discs in their tills will
be unable to get rid of them except by offering to
exchange them at less than their nominal value ;
and, since each disc is necessarily equal in value to
every other disc, everybody else will have to do the
same. The currency of discs has thus become
depreciated. The extent to which it can become
depreciated will depend firstly upon the extent of

the over-issue, and finally upon the metallic value
of the discs. Suppose, for instance, that when the
discs were circulating at their nominal value of one
penny there was room for 1000 of them. Then if
1000 only were issued they would circulate at their
nominal value, however little metal they contained.
If, however, 1200 were issued (the extent of their
circulation being neither increased nor curtailed),
they could not all be absorbed until, on an average,
12 discs were used where 10 discs had been used
before. That is to say, the value of each disc would
have to fall in the ratio of 10 to 12. Even then their
current value might well be greater than their
metallic value, *i.e.* they would still be *token coins*. If
the metallic value of each disc were one farthing,
then, on our previous hypothesis, the current value
of each disc would, after 4000 had been issued, fall
to one farthing also, and become equivalent to its
metallic value. Below this value it could not fall.
The important point to notice is that token coins can
be kept at a current value above that of their metallic
value by a *limitation of issues*. Coins issued without limitation of numbers must circulate at their
metallic value. They become *standard money* ;
though it should be noted that the term *standard*
as thus used has no connotation of excellence either
intrinsic or legal. It is by limitation of issues, and by
limitation of issues only, that a coin, without any

special privileges, can be kept in circulation at a rate higher than that of its metallic value. Limitation of issues, therefore, is essential to a token coinage.

The phrase " without any special privileges " needs explanation. Suppose that our publican when issuing his copper discs (which it should be remembered were of a nominal value equal to one-twelfth of the legal-tender coin) had made a general promise that any person bringing twelve of these discs to the house of issue should get a legal-tender coin in exchange. Then it is obvious that if this promise were kept there could not be an over-issue of discs, for any person finding too many discs in his pocket would but have to go to the issuer and return the surplus discs to him in exchange for legal-tender coin. We have imagined the issue to consist of copper discs, but it might just as well have been composed of pieces of paper. The issue is needed for purposes of exchange, and there is no need that it should have value for any other purpose, provided that, *when not wanted for purposes of exchange*, it can be turned into something which has value for other purposes. It is by thus keeping a store of legal-tender money and redeeming all token or paper money presented by the public that the modern State assures itself against over-issue.

Now to return to the point from which we started.

We have noticed the inconvenience of a system of single legal tender as providing a medium of exchange which is either too cumbersome for large purchases or too valuable for small ones, and have seen how the existence of such a system tends to result in the issue by private persons of subsidiary coins. Such issues inevitably tend to depreciate and to fluctuate in value from day to day. But a fluctuating medium of exchange is a great hindrance to trade, and it has therefore become the custom for civilized communities to abandon the system which leads to such hindrances, and to provide a more flexible currency through the agency of the State. Several systems have been adopted from time to time. Of these the most primitive is the system of *parallel* standards under which the State issues coins of two or more different metals and allows these coins to circulate at their metallic values. When the State goes a step farther and fixes the valency of the coins of different metals—when, for instance, a gold coin is declared by law to be equivalent to 15 silver coins or to 100 copper coins, all coins being equally legal tender—then we have, what was described by the late Professor Jevons, as the *multiple legal tender system*. In practice this system is only important in its simplest form—that of bimetallism—to which reference will be made later. Then there is the system of *composite legal tender*. Under this system coins of one metal are allowed to be standard money, *i.e.* to circulate at their metallic value, and are declared by law to be legal tender, whilst coins of other metals are issued as token coins, *i.e.* the issues are limited so that their current value exceeds their metallic value, and they are declared to be legal tender for small sums only. In England, for instance, the gold sovereign is coined freely, and is allowed to circulate at its metallic value, whilst silver and copper coins are minted in limited quantities, so as to circulate at a scarcity value, and are legal tender to the amount of forty shillings and twelve pence respectively.

Another form of the composite legal-tender system is the *étalon boiteux*, or limping standard, of France. In that country the gold Napoleon is a standard coin freely coined, and the silver *écu* a token coin of restricted issue, but both are legal tender to any amount.

CHAPTER III

HAVING dealt, in the last chapter, with various systems of metallic money, it now remains to consider the subject of bank-notes and cheques. In England the methods of modern banking originated with the goldsmiths of London. The wealthier members of this profession, being necessarily provided with the means of keeping valuables in secure custody, used to undertake the same service for private persons. At first, no doubt, the goldsmiths used to make a charge for this service, but subsequently the profits made by the new business compelled them not only to abolish all charges but even to offer interest on deposits of coin. According to a contemporary pamphlet, the goldsmiths began during the Civil War " to receive the rents of gentlemen's estates remitted to town, and to allow them and others, who put cash into their hands, some interest for it, if it remained but a single month in their hands or even a lesser time. This was a great allurement for people to put money into their hands, which would bear interest till the day they wanted it. And they could also draw it out by £100 or £50 at a time, as they wanted it, with infinitely less trouble than if they had lent it out on either real or personal security. The consequence of it was that it quickly brought a great quantity of cash into their hands ; so that the chief or greatest of them were now enabled to supply Cromwell with money in advance on the revenues as his occasion required upon great advantage to themselves." [1] The notes or receipts given by these goldsmiths for money deposited with them were perhaps the first issues of bank-notes in England. The special importance of such notes lies in the fact that, being the promises of men of known substance and probity, they would, in London at any rate, be universally acceptable at their face value ; could pass from hand to hand in payment, and so fulfil the functions of " money."

Now if we suppose the customers of one of these goldsmiths to have deposited coin to the value of £1000, and the goldsmith to have given in return notes of a similar value, the account of the transaction on the goldsmith's books would be :—

Liabilities.		Assets.	
Notes .	. £1000	Cash .	. £1000

Now it is obvious that if the goldsmith keeps this cash shut up in his coffers he must lose over the transaction, for he is putting himself to the expense

[1] Quoted by Palgrave, Art. " Banks and Banking," *Encyclop. Brit.*

of safeguarding all this gold, and is getting no re-
compense. He is therefore driven to devise some
way of avoiding this loss. Now, the customer who
deposited the £1000 and took notes in exchange
will not want his gold back immediately. Had he
done so he would not have deposited it. He will,
on the contrary, take away the notes and either
keep them in his pocket or use them for making
payments. If he pays them away, the persons to
whom they are paid may either pass them on again
in further payments, or may present them at the
goldsmiths and demand cash. In the ordinary
course of events some persons will pass the notes
on, and others will cash them. The proportion
between the amount kept in circulation and the
amounts cashed will vary from time to time and
under different circumstances, the most important
factors, perhaps, being the demand for paper money
and the reputation of the goldsmith. Whatever the
circumstances, however, provided only that *some*
notes remain in circulation, the goldsmith will find
by experience that he need not keep in his coffers
an amount of cash equal to the whole amount of
notes issued. We may suppose the safe proportion
of cash to notes to be 25 per cent. This being the
case, the goldsmith can issue £4000 in notes for every
£1000 kept in his coffers. He has already given
notes for £1000 to the customer who brought the

gold, and he has therefore £3000 " in hand," so to speak. Supposing any person wants to borrow money, then, the goldsmith will be able to supply him with notes to that amount. These notes, being generally acceptable in payment, will be just as useful to the borrower as cash, and he will be willing to pay interest on the notes given to him. For this sum, however, the borrower will give some sort of security, and the goldsmith's account will then stand as follows :—

Liabilities.		Assets.		
Notes .	. £4000	Cash .	.	£1000
		Securities	.	3000
	£4000			£4000

Out of the interest on the loan of £3000 the goldsmith can pay interest to his depositor and can make a profit for himself. For our present purpose the important point to note is that *a banker makes his profit by adding to the media of circulation.* By so doing he exercises over the development of commerce an influence of the greatest importance.

The new bankers continued to give notes and deposit receipts to their customers until 1781, when cheque-books were substituted. This led to a change in the externals though not in the essentials of banking practice. The London bankers now

practically ceased to issue notes, and instead gave
credit to those who deposited cash, or to those who
borrowed money, by giving them an " account "
and allowing them to draw cheques upon this account
to the amount agreed upon. Let us suppose, as
before, that a customer comes to the bank and
deposits £1000. The banker will then credit that
customer with £1000 on the books of the bank, and
the account of the transaction will be :—

Liabilities.		Assets.	
Deposits of Cus- tomer	£1000	Cash . .	£1000

If, as before, the banker estimates the safe proportion of cash to liabilities as 25 *per cent.*, he will
now be able to make a loan of £3000. Supposing a
borrower, with satisfactory security, to appear, the
banker will credit him with £3000 and give him a
cheque-book. The accounts will now run :—

Liabilities.		Assets.	
Deposits of Cus- tomers	£4000	Cash . .	£1000
		Securities .	3000
	£4000		£4000

It will be seen, then, that there is an essential
similarity between the issue of notes and the granting
of credits. " The essential and distinctive feature

of a ' bank ' and a ' banker ' is to create and issue credit payable on demand, and this credit is intended to be put into circulation and serve all the purposes of money. A bank, therefore, is not an office for borrowing and lending money, but it is a manufactory of credit." " The student must therefore carefully observe that, in the language of banking, *a deposit and an issue are the same thing.* A deposit is simply a credit in a banker's book giving the customer a right of action against him for a sum of money. . . . The word issue comes from *exitus*, a going forth ; and, in mercantile law, to issue an instrument is to deliver it to anyone so as to give him a right of action against the deliverer. . . . When the credit remains in the simple form of a deposit, the banker knows who his creditor is ; when he gives the promissory note, and his creditor transfers it to someone else, the banker has no means of knowing who his creditor is. The same thing, however, may happen in the case of a deposit, because the creditor may transfer his right of action by means of a cheque to anyone else, and it may circulate exactly like a bank note. . . . It is therefore a fundamental error to divide banks into Banks of Deposit and Banks of Issue. All banks are banks of issue." [1]

But, admitting that there is this essential simi-

[1] *Theory and Practice of Banking,* by H. D. Macleod, vol. i. pp. 326-330.

larity between the issue of notes and the creation of deposits, it is necessary also to notice an essential difference, viz., that notes are accepted because of the reputation of the issuing bank, whilst cheques are accepted entirely on the reputation of the drawer.

A poor man presenting a cheque in payment will arouse suspicion, but a bank-note is just as acceptable from a wage-earner as from his employer. Hence notes are better able to circulate amongst the poorer classes than are cheques. Also, since the issue of notes, however small, involves practically no book-keeping, banks will issue small notes where they will not accept small deposits or cash small cheques. For these two reasons, if the issue of small notes is allowed, notes may replace cash in the transactions of the wage-earning classes, whilst the use of cheques, or " deposit-currency," must necessarily be confined almost entirely to the commercial and professional classes. From this follows a most important consequence, viz., that a bank, by issuing small notes, can build up a much greater volume of credit upon a given amount of cash than it could do without the aid of such notes. Let us illustrate this by taking the case of a man who starts business as a banker in an isolated community. Let us suppose that the members of this community entrust him with their gold to the amount of £8000. Then our banker, having £8000 in gold, will be able, as we have seen already, to make loans for a considerably larger amount, say, for six times the amount of gold held by him. But this amount of gold will not be £8000. Whenever a banker makes a loan the borrower may take his money either in the form of a credit on the banker's books, or in large notes, or in cash (including small notes); and thus with increasing loans the cash reserve must necessarily tend to diminish. We may suppose that in the community under consideration the average borrower will take £3 in large notes, or in the form of a credit, for every £1 taken in cash or small notes. Then if our banker be allowed to issue large notes only, his balance-sheet will run as follows :—

Liabilities.		Assets.	
Due to original depositors .	£8,000	Gold . . .	£3,000
Deposit accounts and large notes	10,000	Securities .	15,000
	£18,000		£18,000

That is to say, he has lent £15,000, of which £10,000 has been taken in large notes or as credits on the bank's books, and of which £5000 has been taken in cash, leaving a balance of £3000 in gold as a reserve. But, were the banker able to issue small notes as well as large ones, it might well be that loans to the

c

amount of £15,000 would involve a withdrawal of only £3000 in gold, the other £2000 being taken in small notes. The banker would then be able to make other loans to the amount of £12,000 whilst still preserving a ratio of cash to liabilities of one-sixth.

Liabilities.		Assets.	
Original Depositors	£8,000	Gold .	£5,000
Deposit accounts			
and large notes	20,000	Securities	25,000
Small notes . .	2,000		
	£30,000		£30,000

We see, therefore, that although it is true that all banks are banks of issue, yet there is an important difference between deposit currency and notes, especially small notes. It is owing to this difference that nearly every civilized State has passed laws regulating the issue of notes, whilst the regulation of deposit currency is almost unknown.

Let us first deal with the regulation of note issues. This regulation may be accomplished either by the passing of laws conditioning the issue of notes by private institutions, or by the adoption of the function of note issue by the State itself. The latter is the more common course in countries where the use of notes is a recent development, but unfortunately it has been frequently abused. A State which issues notes can declare those notes to be legal tender, and can thus force its subjects to accept them in payment. Thus a deficit in revenue can be filled merely by the printing of more notes, a course which almost inevitably leads to excessive issues. Before passing from this point, however, it may be useful to consider more carefully what is meant by an " excessive " issue. To deal with this question at length would involve a study of the subject of foreign exchange—a subject which is outside the scope of this book. Here it must be sufficient to compare all countries using the same standard of value to a series of upright cylinders open at the top end and closed at the bottom, each cylinder being connected with every other by a pipe. Then if water be poured into the whole system to represent the money material, this water will distribute itself amongst the cylinders so that each cylinder contains a volume of water proportionate to the area of its end. Similarly, the money material of the world distributes itself among the different countries in amounts proportionate to the trade of each country, in such a way as to keep the level of prices (represented by the level of water) the same in every country thus connected. Thus the quantity of money in a country may be said to be excessive not when it is large *absolutely*, but when it is large relatively to the amount of money in other countries having the same volume of trade. The existence of an excess of money in any country is to be deduced not from the fact that the amount of money in that country is large, but from the fact that the level of prices is higher than in other countries. The consequence of a relatively high level of prices in any country is that money material tends to flow into other countries, just as water tends to seek its level. Such an outward flow, or the tendency towards such a flow, is manifested by an "unfavourable exchange." If we imagine a group of countries all using gold as their medium of exchange, and then suppose that one of these countries undertakes the issue of paper money, the following train of consequences will ensue :—The country of issue, *ex hypothesi*, will already have its due quota of gold, so that an issue of paper money will displace some of this gold and cause it to flow to other countries. The paper money, it should be noted, cannot flow out, for it would not be accepted in payment by the people of other countries. Therefore, as more and more paper is issued, the money of this country will come to contain less and less gold. Finally, when all the gold has been driven out, the currency of the country concerned will be increased by the gross amount of all fresh issues of paper, prices will rise rapidly, and the foreign exchanges will fall to a corresponding level. The evils of such conditions are amongst the common-places of finance.

In order to avoid the dangers of over-issue most States have adopted some system whereby the issue of notes becomes more or less automatic in its character. The Government of India, for instance, issues notes up to a certain limit against securities, and for every note issued beyond that limit holds an equivalent of metal. From time to time, as the note circulation expands, the " fiduciary " portion, *i.e.* the portion issued against securities, is increased by Statute.

In the case of private issues the dangers of mis-management are not so great, because no private institution can make its notes legal tender, and so compel persons to receive them. All economists have agreed, of course, that note-issuing institutions require careful management. Even Adam Smith based his disapproval of the circulation of small notes on the ground that, by issuing such notes, any petty tradesman was enabled to set up as a banker. But there is a further point around which raged a most famous controversy—the controversy between the " Banking " school and the " Currency " school. The former school, represented by Thomas Tooke and M. Chevalier, and supported by the authority of Adam Smith, maintained that, provided the issuers of notes were sound men, always prepared to redeem their notes in gold when asked to do so, then they might be allowed to issue notes freely without danger of inflation. The Currency school, led by Lord Overstone in England and M. Wolowski in France, objected that " there is a liability to excessive issues of paper even while that paper is convertible at will," and demanded that the privilege of note issue should be restricted to a single institution and subjected to considerable limitations. This controversy is not of great theoretical value, inasmuch as neither party sufficiently realized that " all banks are banks of issue." In practice, however, it is interesting to note that the currency principle has been triumphant in Europe.

In England, since 1844, the privilege of note issue has been practically confined to the Bank of England, subject also to the limitation that all notes issued beyond a certain limit shall be backed by an amount of gold equal to the face value of the notes so issued. The total amount of the issue, however, is not limited. In Germany there are, besides the Reichsbank, three other banks of issue, but their issues are small. The Reichsbank has a practical monopoly. It may issue notes against the following assets :—First, the amount of specie—gold, copper, silver and nickel—and of gold bullion held by the bank ; second, the amount of government notes so held ; third, the amount of notes of other banks held by the Reichsbank ; fourth, approved bills of exchange to a fixed amount—this amount being known as the *Kontingent*. The issue against bills may be increased beyond the amount of the *Kontingent*, subject to a tax of 5 *per cent.* on the face value of the excess issue, and subject also to the limitation that the total issues must not be greater than three times the amount of gold, silver, copper, and nickel specie, of gold bullion, and of government notes held by the bank.

In France the Bank of France has the monopoly of issue, and may issue notes in discount of approved bills or in loans without any compulsory backing of metal. The total issue is limited, but the limit is a wide one and is enlarged from time to time. In 1906 it was fixed at 5,800 millions of francs. Within this limit, however, the French issue is managed on banking rather than on currency principles. " When circumstances demand a reduction of issue the notes are presented naturally for redemption, and it seems to us that so long as this redemption is made without difficulty there can never be any excess of notes in circulation. . . . It is the bills presented and the requests for loans which regulate automatically the movements of issue." [1]

[1] *Interviews on Banking and Currency Systems*, U.S.A. Senate, Doc. 405, 1910. This might almost be an extract from the evidence of the Bank of England directors before the Bullion Committee of 1810.

Now, with regard to the regulation of deposit currency. We have seen that in many ways the creation of deposit currency resembles the issue of paper money. Whilst, however, it is usual to regulate carefully the issue of notes, the creation of deposit currency is generally allowed to proceed without restriction. But two prominent exceptions occur in the case of Belgium and the United States. In Belgium a reserve of gold and gold bills equivalent to one-third of note issues *plus* deposits is required. In the United States banks are made to keep a reserve of gold varying from 15 to 25 *per cent.* of their deposits.

Whether the regulation of deposits is desirable is a question of great practical interest, the discussion of which requires, as a preliminary, a more detailed consideration of the matter of bank reserves. I propose to consider, therefore (1) what proportion of reserves to deposits should be kept by a prudent banker, and (2) whether bankers should be compelled to maintain this proportion at all times. As to the first question it must be admitted at once that the quantity of gold, or of other legal-tender metal, which should be kept by a banker, must be primarily determined by practical experience. But a few hints may be obtained from theory. " A bank whose [deposit currency] circulates among a rural population, going twenty or fifty miles from the place

of issue, where intelligence of disaster would make
its way slowly, is in a very different position from
one whose [deposit currency] is mainly held in the
city where it is issued. Here the whole population
can be brought into the streets by the stroke of a bell ;
intelligence of evil spreads rapidly, and the contagion
of panic acts with terrific force." [1] A banker,
therefore, who serves a small but populous area
should, *other things being equal*, keep a larger cash
reserve than he who serves a scattered country
district. A further point is that banks may safely
keep a smaller reserve if they agree to pool their
resources, either directly or indirectly. To illustrate
this point let us take the case of a country having
only two banks. Let these two banks divide the
business equally between them, and let each bank
keep the same proportion of cash as the other. At
any given moment suppose their balance-sheets to
show the following figures :—

Liabilities.			Assets.			
Deposits . .	£100		Loans	. . .	£90
			Cash	. . .	10
	£100				£100

Now, if a financial panic arise, there will be, as one

[1] *Money*, by F. A. Walker, p. 413. Mr Walker intended his remarks
to apply to reserves held against notes, but they apply equally to
reserves held against deposits.

result, a general demand for gold. Persons who have usually paid their debts by cheque may be obliged to pay in gold, and will have to withdraw some of their deposits for that purpose. The balance-sheets of the banks will show a change for the worse, thus :—

Liabilities.			Assets.			
Deposits	. .	£95	Loans	. . .	£90
			Cash	. . .	5
		£95			£95

Owing to the diminution of their cash reserves the banks will be disinclined to grant any further credits. Indeed they will rather be inclined to restrict those already granted. Suppose that a business man, in urgent need of a loan, applies to Bank A for the money, the bank may have to refuse, even if it knows that such a refusal may ruin the would-be borrower, and so precipitate a panic. For if it grants the loan what happens ? The borrower draws a cheque on Bank A in favour of some person who may be a customer of Bank B. If the payee of the cheque then gives it to Bank B for collection, this bank will demand payment of the cheque from Bank A—payment in gold. If such payment be very large it is obvious that Bank A may be drained of the whole of its already small cash balance, and may be obliged to close its doors. Therefore, if Bank A gives the required loan, it may ruin itself; if it refuses the loan it may ruin its customer and precipitate a panic. Had there been only *one bank* in the country, however, this dilemma would have been avoided. The payee of the cheque would have paid it *into the same bank which granted the loan*, and no gold would have been put into motion. Supposing the loan to be £3, the only change would be an increase of loans and of deposits, thus :—

Liabilities.			Assets.			
Deposits	.	. £98	Loans	.	. .	£93
			Gold	.	. .	5
		£98				£98

It is impossible, of course, to arrange for the amalgamation of all the banks of a country into one institution, but, without any such drastic change, similar benefits may be obtained by an indirect pooling of reserves. In Europe this pooling has taken the form of " central discounting institutions," such as the Banks of England and France. These institutions are used as " banker's banks," in which the other banks deposit a large part of their spare cash. Let us pursue our former illustration and suppose that, besides the Banks A and B, there is in our imaginary country a central Bank C. In this bank both A and B will keep deposits, and any

balance which may be due from A to B, or from B
to A, will be settled by adjustments in the books of
Bank C. If Bank A has been lending freely there
will probably arise, as we have already seen, a
balance in favour of Bank B which may finally
reduce the account of Bank A on the books of Bank
C to dangerously small dimensions. But the total
cash at Bank C will be unaffected by such changes.
Bank C, therefore, will not require Bank A to
replenish its balance with cash ; it will merely ask
for securities, such as bills of exchange, and will
credit the value of these to Bank A. But Bank A
will already have in its portfolio the bills against
which it has made loans, and these bills it will be
able to pass on to Bank C, in return for the credit
which that bank has given. This is the device of
rediscounting, and is equivalent to an indirect
pooling of reserves.

In America there are no such central institutions
as we have here imagined, but the device of " clearing-house certificates " has been used as a temporary
measure. Under this system it is agreed by a group
of bankers using a common clearing-house that any
bank depositing an adequate margin of securities
with the clearing-house shall be entitled to a certificate, which certificate may be used in payment
of balances due to other banks of the same group.
This is, in effect, a system of rediscounting, and pro-

duces the same result ; that is, it enables individual banks to lend freely without fear of finding their cash balances gone.

We may now see that legislation, which compels every bank to keep a fixed proportion of cash to liabilities, renders difficult, if not impossible, any such pooling of reserves as has just been described. The results of past American legislation have been acutely paralleled by Mr Warburg. " If after a prolonged drought a thunderstorm threatens, what would be the consequence if the wise mayor of a town should attempt to meet the danger of fire by distributing the available water, giving to each house-owner one pailful ? When the lightning strikes, the unfortunate householder will in vain fight the fire with his one pailful of water, while the other citizens will all frantically hold on to their own little supply, their only defence in face of danger. The fire will spread, and resistance will be impossible. If, however, instead of uselessly dividing the water, it had remained concentrated in one reservoir, with an effective system of pipes to direct it where it was wanted for short energetic and efficient use, the town would have been safe." [1] Since the American financial crisis of 1907 the regulation of deposits has been universally discredited.

[1] *The Discount System in Europe*, p. 33, U.S.A. Senate, Doc. No. 402, 1910.

CHAPTER IV

THE EQUATION OF EXCHANGE

WE have seen that the primary function of a
" money " is to act as the medium of exchange.
An equally important function is that of acting
as a common measure of value ; and it is that
function which we have now to consider. In the
first place, it is important to notice that the value of
goods as measured in money, or, indeed, in any
other way, is relative only. If the " money " be
gold, and the unit of money one ounce, and if a suit
of clothes exchanges for one ounce of gold, and a
carpet for two ounces, we may say that the value of
a suit of clothes is *one* and of a carpet *two* ounces of
gold. But what is the value of an ounce of gold ?
Adam Smith has answered this question by saying
that " labour . . . is the real measure of value
both of [gold] and of all other commodities." [1]
According to Adam Smith, then, the value of an
ounce of gold is to be measured by the amount of
labour which it will buy. The wages of a skilled
labourer are composed in part of interest on the
capital sunk in his education ; but the wages of an

[1] *Wealth of Nations*, Bk. II., c. xi Part III.

unskilled labourer represent the reward of " labour " only, so far as such a thing as pure " labour " can be postulated. If a given amount of labour be admitted as the measure of intrinsic disutility, then the reward necessary to evoke that amount of labour may be taken as the measure of absolute utility, or value. In so far, then, as an hour of pure labour remains equally disagreeable to mankind, as represented by the unskilled labourer, so long we may suppose the reward given for such a quantity of labour will remain of the same absolute value. Upon this hypothesis, if the average hourly wage in any given year be 6d., and in another year 12d., it would be reasonable to say that the value of money has fallen 50 *per cent.* in the interval. But in this solution of the difficulty there are two flaws. First, the practical difficulty that the disutility of an hour's unskilled labour will vary with the intensity of the work, and intensity of work can hardly be measured. Unskilled labour may vary from the intense application of the English navvy to the desultory loitering of the Indian mill-hand. It would not be fair to assume that the disutility of an hour's work would be the same in both cases. Therefore, even if the truth of Adam Smith's theory be admitted, its practical application would be impossible. Secondly, there is the more essential difficulty that, even if we suppose the intensity of labour to remain the same,

the disutility of labour may vary.   Education, giving
increased stimulus to the enjoyment of leisure ; the
spread of democratic ideas, bringing increased self-
respect ;   these, and many other causes, may influence man's attitude towards labour, and cause an
hour's labour to be more (or less) distasteful to him.
The disutility of labour, in fact, may vary in time
and place, and it is not admissible to assume that
a given amount of labour can be used as the unit
of *absolute* disutility.   It would seem, then, that
Adam Smith's suggestion for a measure of absolute
value, however reasonable at first sight, cannot be
accepted on further analysis.   Value, as J. B. Say
has said, is a " moral quality " and is not susceptible
of treatment other than that which can be applied
to such qualities.   We must therefore give up the
attempt to discover any absolute measure of the
value of money, and be content with a more liminal
view.

Let us return, now, to our former supposition.
We had supposed that an ounce of gold was the
measure of value, and that the value of a suit of
clothes was one, and of a carpet two ounces of gold.
Then since the value of a carpet is two ounces, the
value of an ounce of gold may equally well be said
to be half a carpet.   The value of money, that is to
say, consists in what it will buy, *i.e.* in its purchasing
power.   If the value of a carpet were to sink to half

an ounce of gold, the value of gold, so far as purchasing carpets is concerned, will have doubled. The purchasing power of money obviously varies inversely as the level of prices, so that when the value, or purchasing power, of money rises the level of prices must fall, and *vice versa.*

Having thus dealt very shortly with the connection between the value of money and the level of prices, I propose to turn to what is perhaps the most interesting and important question of monetary science —the relation between the level of prices and the quantity of money in circulation.

To attack this question in its most simple form let us suppose a communistic State composed of 100 members, and let us suppose further that these members are supplied freely with shelter and clothing, but are allowed to purchase their food at State shops, with counters issued to them daily in payment for their day's work. Under such conditions the State will have so to adjust the daily wage, and the price of food at the shops, that each member may be able to buy an adequate daily ration of food and drink. If the number of tokens given daily to each person be 10, and the number of individuals be 100, then the number of tokens paid out every evening will be 1000. In such case 1000 tokens will be tendered daily at the State shops in exchange for 100 rations, and the average price of

D

each ration will be 10.   If the daily wage for any
reason be reduced to 5 tokens, there will be only 500
tokens tendered daily in exchange for 100 rations,
and the average price of a ration will sink to 5.   Thus
the price of rations will vary directly with the amount
of tokens in circulation.   But there is still another
factor to be considered.   If it be the custom to spend
wages the same evening that they are received, and
if the shops are able to return these tokens promptly
to the wage-paying office, it will be possible to pay
out the same tokens next evening, so that the total
number of tokens required by the State will be only
1000 (if we assume a daily wage of 10).   If, however,
the wage-earners are more deliberate in getting rid
of their tokens, it may be that two days, or even
three days, will elapse before the tokens have com-
pleted their round from the wage-paying office to
the wage-earner, from the wage-earner to the shop,
and from the shop to the wage office.   If two days be
the time required for circulation, then two complete
sets of tokens, or 2000 in all, will be required ; if
three days, then 3000, and so on.   The slower the
velocity of circulation the more tokens will have to
be kept in circulation if the same level of prices is to
be maintained.   But if the number of tokens in
circulation be kept the same, any decline in the
velocity of circulation must cause a fall in the level
of prices.   If 1000 tokens be in use, the time of

circulation being one day, the daily wage and the price of a ration will be 10. If, however, the time of circulation be two days, the daily wage and the price of a ration will be 5. We see, therefore, that the price of rations varies directly as the rapidity of circulation of the tokens. It is further obvious that if, instead of 100 rations, 200 were made available every day, the price of each ration would fall by half, since the number of tokens offered would remain the same. That is, the price of each ration will, *ceteris paribus,* vary inversely as the number of rations sold. These relations between the price of goods, the quantity of goods, the quantity of money, and its velocity of circulation have been expressed in an equation, generally known as the " equation of exchange." Thus, if M be the quantity of tokens, V the number of times which the tokens are exchanged against goods in one day, P the price of each ration, and R the number of rations sold in one day, we have the relation

$$MV = RP$$

This equation is the simplest expression of the " quantity theory " in its modern form, *i.e.* the theory that, other things being equal, the level of prices (P) will vary with the quantity of money in use (M). In a sense this equation represents a truism, for if M be the number of coins of unit value in circulation, and V be the average number of times which each coin is used during any given period for purposes of exchange, MV must be equal to the money spent by buyers during that period. And if R be the number of goods sold during that period, and P the average price paid, RP must be equal to the money received by sellers. And this must, obviously, be equal to MV, the money spent by buyers. But, though the equation of exchange may seem to state merely what everybody knew before, it is nevertheless a powerful instrument of correct thinking, and will repay the most diligent attention.

The above is a simple and generalized form of the equation of exchange, both on the money and on the goods side. In real life R will represent, not one single commodity as we have imagined here, but an indefinite number of commodities, each with its own price, and the equation will be—

$$MV = R_1P_1 + R_2P_2 + R_3P_3$$

For the present, however, we will retain the single letter R as representing "goods in general," while P denotes the "level of prices."

But the money side of the equation also needs expansion. So far we have supposed M to represent money in the form of coin and notes. In modern commerce, however, goods are bought not only with coin, but also, and to a much larger extent with cheques, and the element of cheques must therefore be taken into consideration. A cheque, as we have seen, is simply a document by which is transferred the right to credit with a banker. Such credits can be used as a medium of exchange, and the total amount of " current accounts," or " deposits subject to cheque," represents the amount of this medium. Let this amount be represented by M′, and the average velocity of circulation of these rights by V′. Then the equation becomes

$$MV + M'V' = RP,$$

showing that an increase in the total of current accounts, or an increase in the velocity of circulation of the rights thereto, will lead to a rise of prices in just the same way as an increase in the amount of coin or of *its* velocity of circulation.

Since the variations of M′ have this important effect upon prices, it will be necessary to consider shortly the causes which lead to such variations. In the first place, then, it is obvious that current accounts presuppose banks, and that the more numerous and widely distributed are these banks the more persons will be able to take advantage of them. Next to the existence of banks the development of the " cheque habit "—to use a convenient Americanism—is the most vital factor in the growth of current accounts. Persons who wish to draw cheques must open current accounts, and, therefore, the more commonly cheques are used, the larger, other things being equal, will be the sum total of current accounts. Thus the growth of intelligence and initiative amongst the wage-earning class will lead to the extended use of banking facilities, and hence to the growth of current accounts. Another important factor affecting the growth of the cheque habit is the system of "shop credit." When the retail shops begin to open accounts with their customers instead of asking for cash down, those customers who keep banking accounts, instead of carrying about in their pockets, as formerly, such cash as is required for everyday purchases, will leave the money at their bankers, and will settle for these purchases with a periodical cheque ; whilst those customers who do not keep banking accounts will be encouraged to open such accounts. Any system, in fact, which substitutes large payments for small ones will encourage the multiplication of current accounts. Even a general rise of prices will have some influence in this direction by enabling persons, who before the rise could not keep the minimum balance, to increase their assets sufficiently to comply with the rules of the bank.

But the banks themselves have a large influence in affecting the growth of current accounts. In the first place, they may encourage the use of cheques by taking small accounts and allowing the drawing of cheques for small sums. A badly-paid clerk will not be able to open an account with a minimum balance of £20, nor would any account be of much use to him were he not allowed to draw small cheques. In the United States where, owing to keen competition, banks are willing to oblige small customers, cheques are sometimes drawn for 50 or 25 cents, and occasionally even for less ; and it has been estimated that 80 to 88 *per cent.* of all sale transactions are effected by means of cheques.[1] Secondly, bankers may encourage the growth of current accounts by granting loans on easy terms. We have seen that a loan granted by a bank usually takes the form of a credit on the bank's books against which the borrower may draw cheques. But the power of the banker, thus to alter the total of current accounts, is a limited one. Current accounts imply a liability on the part of the banker to pay gold on demand, and he must therefore keep a supply of gold to meet any such demand which may arise. The ratio of gold to liabilities is one which will vary at different times and in different banks. " Some banks are more cautiously conducted than others and show a higher proportion of cash to liabilities, but, broadly speaking, bankers as a body

[1] *The Use of Credit Instruments in the U.S.,* by Dr Kinley, p. 10.

will not allow this proportion to fall below a certain figure. The most daring of bankers will cease to lend when his cash reserve has fallen beyond a certain point. On the other hand, the most cautious will increase his loans when cash becomes abundant in his vaults. Thus it becomes evident that the superstructure of credit cannot be indefinitely increased or decreased without any reference to the cash basis upon which it rests, but that, within certain broad limits, which will vary with the state of credit and the general organization of commerce, it must depend upon and vary with the size of that cash basis."

Before passing from this point we may point out the distinction between an increase of cheques *at the expense of* metallic money, and an increase of cheques which *accompanies* an increase of metallic money in use. Normally, in any given country and at any given time, the transactions effected by cheque will bear a more or less definite proportion to the transactions effected by cash. "Individual firms and corporations preserve more or less definite ratios between their cash transactions and their cheque transactions. These ratios are determined by motives of individual convenience and habit. In general business firms use money for wage payments, and for small miscellaneous transactions under the term 'petty cash'; while for settle-

ment with each other they usually prefer cheques.
These preferences are so strong that we could not
imagine them over-ridden except temporarily and
to a small degree. A business firm would hardly
pay car-fares with cheques and liquidate its large
liabilities with cash. Each person strikes an equilibrium between his use of the two methods of payment and does not greatly disturb it except for short
periods of time. . . . Whenever his stock of money
becomes relatively small, and his bank balance
relatively large, he cashes a cheque. In the opposite
event he deposits cash. In this way he is constantly converting one of the two media of exchange
into the other. A private individual usually feeds
his purse from his bank account ; a retail commercial firm usually feeds its bank account from
its till. The bank acts as intermediary for both." [1]
Normally, then, any changes in the extent of the cash
circulation, MV, will be accompanied by concomi-
tant changes in the extent of the cheque circulation,
M'V', and the ratio of these two quantities will not
vary. Changes in this ratio may, however, be brought
about by such developments as the extension of
banking facilities or the growth of the cheque habit.

The luminous passage which we have just quoted
calls attention to a most important point, viz., the
force of custom in keeping the amount of cheque

[1] *The Purchasing Power of Money*, by Prof. Irving Fisher, p. 50.

circulation in a definite ratio to the amount of money circulation. It is a commonplace, and not a very sound commonplace, of economics that the amount of deposit currency is kept at a more or less definite ratio to the amount of available cash, because bankers are compelled to keep a reserve against their liabilities. And even Professor Irving Fisher bows the knee to this idol of the theatre. Analysis shows, however, that the force of custom, which maintains the ratio of cash transactions to cheque transactions, is far the most powerful factor in maintaining the ratio of cash to deposit currency, and is entirely independent of any considerations of bankers' reserves.[1]

We have not yet analysed the causes which control the amount of M—the money in circulation —and it is to this important and complicated problem that we must now address ourselves. Let us suppose an isolated country supplied with gold from its own mines, and further, that the currency of this country is composed entirely of gold and of deposit currency based upon gold. Let us further suppose that there is gratuitous coinage of gold at an open mint, *i.e.* that any quantity of gold brought to the mint will be coined free of cost to the bringer. Under such circumstances an ounce of gold just brought from the

[1] See Appendix B.

mines may be used with equal ease for making coins or for making ornaments. Similarly, gold in the form of ornaments may be melted down and made into coin without expense, whilst gold in the form of coin may without loss be used for making ornaments. This being the case, it is obvious that gold coin must be equal in value to the same weight of gold ornaments, allowance being made, of course, for the cost of workmanship. Apart from this cost of workmanship, then, the price of gold ornaments, as measured in gold coin, cannot vary.

Now let us consider the demand for gold. This demand may be split up into three portions. First, a demand for gold coin for circulation ; second, a demand for gold, either as coin or bullion, to be placed in bankers' reserves as a basis for deposit currency ; and, third, a demand for non-monetary uses, which we may summarize as a demand for gold ornaments. We have already seen how, with a given development of business organization, the use of coin tends to bear a more or less fixed ratio to the use of deposit currency, that is how

$$M'V' = a\ MV,$$

where a is a constant. If we further assume V' and V to remain constant, and at worst they are very slowly changing quantities, we get

$$M' = b\ M,$$

where b is another constant. That is to say, the amount of deposit currency, in any given *conjuncture*, is a definite multiple of the amount of cash in circulation. But, as we have shown before, bankers tend to keep a more or less steady ratio of reserve to deposits, say of $1/c$. That is,

$$\text{reserve} \times c = \text{M}'.$$
But, $$\text{M}' = b\ \text{M}.$$

Therefore, $$\text{reserve} = \frac{b}{c}\ \text{M}.$$

where $\frac{b}{c}$ is constant. We may therefore say that, at any given stage of business development, the demand for gold for bankers' reserves will bear a fixed ratio to the demand for gold for circulation. It will be admissible, then, to combine the first two of the three demands and to classify the demand for gold as " monetary " and " non-monetary." The total supply of available gold will then be devoted to satisfying these two demands, and will be divided between the two uses in such a way that the final utility of an ounce of gold in each use will be the same. Thus any invention or change of fashion which causes an increased flow of gold to non-monetary uses will *pro tanto* diminish the supply available for monetary uses, whilst an increased demand for coin, arising out of a greater volume of exchanges, will be satisfied by an influx of gold which would otherwise have been used for ornamental or other artistic purposes. But, except in very exceptional cases, an increased supply of gold will go partly into one use, partly into the other. We see then that M, the amount of gold coin in circulation, depends, first, on the total available stock of gold, and, second, on the ratio of the intensities of the demands for gold for monetary and for non - monetary purposes.

The above analysis disposes of certain recent criticisms which have been directed against the quantity theory of money. These criticisms are to the following effect :—According to the *classical* quantity theory prices depend upon the quantity of metallic money in existence. If you attempt to show that prices vary with the quantity of metallic money *plus* the quantity of deposit currency, you are setting up an entirely new doctrine. If you still defend the classical theory, and base your argument upon the quantity of metallic money alone, what do you mean by " quantity " ? Do you mean the quantity of money in circulation, the quantity of bankers' reserves, or both ? Now we have seen that, roughly speaking, at any given phase of commercial development, the amount of deposit currency will be a constant multiple of the

metal in circulation, and that the amount of
metal in circulation will be a constant multiple
of the metal in bankers' reserves. Those quantities, in fact, which our critics have put for-
ward as independent, are really interdependent,
and we may say indifferently that the course of
prices will vary, other things being equal (1)
with the total amount of circulating media (deposit and metallic), (2) with the total amount of
circulating metal, or (3) with the total amount
of circulating metal *plus* the metal in bankers'
reserves.

It may perhaps be helpful to illustrate, by means
of an hydraulic model, the phenomena which have
just been described. Let us imagine, then, two
cylinders, A and B (see Fig. 1), open at the top and
closed at the bottom. Let these cylinders be connected (1) by a pipe, C D, passing from the bottom
of A to the bottom of B, and (2) by an open trough,
E F, passing from the top of A to the top of B.
Let water be poured into this system until the
cylinders, the pipe, and the trough be filled to a
level pp'. In the pipe C D, at the point c, let there
be a screw caused to revolve by power outside the
cylinder in such a way that, when so revolved, it
causes the water to circulate through the system
at an even rate. Above this system let there be
two endless bands, T and T', revolving with their

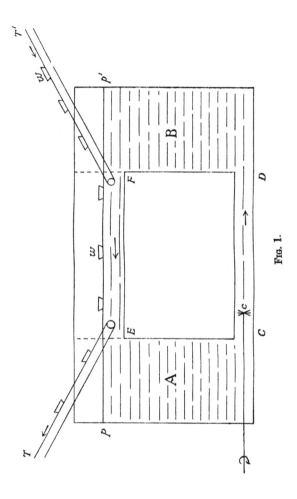

Fig. 1.

ends slightly below the water at E and F. On the band T′ let there be placed at regular intervals little blocks of wood, w, w - - -, so that as the band revolves these blocks are cast upon the water at F. Then since the water is being driven round the system by the screw at c, the blocks of wood will be carried along by the water until they reach E. Here they will be caught up on the other revolving band T, and carried out of the system.

On this model the cylinders A and B represent banks, the water represents the money in circulation, the small blocks of wood represent commodities, and the carriage of these blocks from F to E represents the exchange of commodities against money. The velocity with which the water flows along the trough F E represents the velocity of circulation of money, and the frequency with which blocks are brought down on to the water by the band T′ represents the volume of trade. The level of prices will then be represented by the total volume of water in the trough E F, divided by the number of blocks of wood actually floating thereupon, *i.e.* by the average volume of water which may be considered as devoted to the carriage of each block.

Let us now consider the changes which would be brought about in this system by variations of its different elements. In the first place, then, as to the velocity of circulation of the water. If the velocity of flow be such that each block of wood takes one minute to pass from F to E, and if six blocks are brought down by the band T' in one minute, it is obvious that the total number of blocks in transit on the water at any given instant will be six. If the velocity of flow of the water be then increased so that each block takes only half a minute in passing from F to E, and if still six blocks a minute are brought down by T', the total number of blocks on the water at any instant will be three. The volume of water devoted to each block will thus be doubled, i.e. the level of prices will be doubled. Similarly, if the velocity of flow of the water be halved, other things remaining the same, the number of blocks simultaneously in transit on the water will be doubled, i.e. the price level will be halved.

Secondly, we have to consider changes in the amount of water in the system, i.e. changes in the amount of money in the country. Here it is obvious that an increase of water will raise the level of the water in the trough F E. If the velocity of the water remains the same, this rise of level will give a greater volume of water to each block carried, i.e. prices will rise. It must be noted, however, that if more water be poured into the

E

model, whilst the driving power of the screw at c remains constant, there will be a fall in the velocity of flow of water along the trough F E.   From this it might appear that an increase in the total quantity of money affects its velocity of circulation, or, as Sir William Petty said, that " money is but the fat of the body politic whereof too much doth often hinder its activity as too little makes it sick." This, however, as will be seen later, is a false analogy, and the model must be so arranged that for every increase or decrease of water the power at c is so altered as to keep the water in F E flowing at the same velocity.   This arrangement having been made, any increase or decrease of water will imply a larger or smaller volume of water to carry each block, $i.e.$ an increase in the quantity of money in circulation will raise prices, whilst a decrease will lower prices.   We need not tie ourselves down to any quantitative relation between the total amount of money in the country, and the level of prices. It will be sufficient to specify that the trough F E be a rectangular one, so that the level of ‵prices will vary directly with the amount of money in active circulation, $i.e.$ which is being actually used for effecting exchanges.   The water in the cylinders A and B may be regarded as money in the coffers of banks, whilst the water in the tube C D represents money in transit between banks.

Lastly, as to changes in the volume of trade. The volume of trade, as has already been said, is represented by the number of blocks brought down in a given time by the band T'. The greater the number of these the greater will be the volume of trade, and *vice versa*. The greater the number of blocks which are cast on to the trough at F in any given time, the greater, other things being equal, will be the total number of blocks in transit from F to E ; the smaller will be the volume of water allotted to each block, and the lower will be the level of prices.

Another point which deserves attention at this stage is the conception of coin circulating between banks, as shown on the model. Usually coins are pictured as passing continually from hand to hand in payment for goods or otherwise, and only entering a bank incidentally and occasionally. And this may be the case sometimes with individual coins. But if we look at the price paid rather than at the coins used ; if, for instance, when a four-shilling good is purchased with a crown piece, we look at the increase of four shillings in the trader's till, rather than at the crown piece given and the shilling received as change, we shall see that there is considerable truth in the conception of money emerging from a bank, being exchanged against goods or services and then entering the same or another bank *before* being again used for another exchange. Let us take, for instance, the common case of a professional man who withdraws from his bank cash to be used for current expenses. This will pass into the till of the trader from whom goods are bought, and then, so far as that trader banks his receipts and does not use them to meet expenses, the money will pass into a bank again, having accomplished one exchange during its temporary outing. This process represents a large class of expenditure, but there is another important class of expenditure which takes a different form. I refer to the payment of wages. If a trader draws cash from his bank wherewith to pay wages, this cash will first pass to the wage-earners in exchange for services, from the wage-earners it will pass to the shopkeepers in exchange for goods, and from the shopkeepers it will pass again to the banks, having accomplished two exchanges in transit. Of course this is only a rough generalization. A considerable part of a shopkeeper's receipts, instead of being banked, may be used for meeting expenses. A part, though probably a small part, of wages earned may be used by the earners for purposes other than the purchasing of goods. Still, subject to these limitations, it may be said that money drawn out from banks to be used for wage payments affects two exchanges before passing into a bank again, whilst money drawn out to be used for other payments circulates only once in transit. The value of this generalization, which we owe to the brilliant analysis of Professor Irving Fisher, will be seen in the next chapter.

CHAPTER V

VELOCITY OF CIRCULATION

WE have now to deal in more detail with the concept of velocity of circulation. This factor of our equation, owing to the comparative smallness of its variations and the apparent impossibility of their measurement, has only of recent years attracted the attention which it deserves. It is, however, of great importance to the student to realize fully the significance of such variations, in order that his attention may not be monopolized by the larger and more striking changes which occur in the volume of trade or the amount of currency. I propose, therefore, to touch first upon the meaning of the term, velocity of circulation, then upon the causes which affect this velocity, and, finally, upon the methods by which it may be measured. First, then, as to the meaning of the term. If the unit of time be a year, it might be supposed that the velocity of circulation would be measured by the average number of times which each coin changed hands during a year. This supposition, however, is wrong in two respects. In the first place a coin of large value is of more importance than a small

70

one. The valency of a sovereign, for instance, which changes hands 16 times a year may be represented by 320 (20 × 16), whilst the valency of a shilling circulating 20 times a year will be represented by 20. That is to say, when taking an average, the velocity of each coin must be weighted by its value. In the second place, since velocity of circulation is of importance chiefly as affecting the purchasing power of money, we must take account only of such sums as change hands in payment for goods. Not only should all money given or lent be excluded, but also all money paid in excess of the price of the articles bought, and all money returned as " change." If, for instance, the price of an article be two shillings, and the purchaser tender half-a-crown, the effective transfer is of two shillings only. The excess sixpence paid, and returned as change, must be disregarded.

Owing to these two considerations the conception of velocity of circulation, as reached in this way, appears somewhat artificial. It may be useful, therefore, to consider it from another point of view —from the point of view, that is, of the spender, not from the point of view of the individual coin. In this way the velocity of circulation is measured by the average rate of turn-over of the pocket-money of individual spenders. Thus if A, the " average man," keeps, on an average, forty shillings in his pocket or his purse, and pays out cash at the rate of twenty shillings a week, he will pay out during the year 20×52 shillings, and his rate of cash turn-over will be $\dfrac{20 \times 52}{40}$, or 26. By this method we escape the necessity of referring to any excess tendered, or returned as change. We do not escape, however, the necessity of excepting all cash paid out in gifts or in loans. Nevertheless, from this point of view the conception of velocity of circulation is considerably simplified, and is, moreover, reduced to a form in which its magnitude may be roughly estimated.

Before passing from this subject it will be necessary to extend the above considerations from coin and notes to the case of deposit currency. As in the case of coin and notes, we obtained a measure of the rate of turn-over by weighing the average sum kept in the purse against the annual cash expenditure, so, in the case of deposit currency, we may measure this quantity by weighing the average current account kept at the bank against the annual payments by cheque. Thus, if a man's average current account be £100, and he writes cheques every year to the total of £5000, the rate of turn-over, or velocity of circulation, of his deposit currency will be $\dfrac{5000}{100}$, or 50. The average of such velocities over the whole banking community, weighted, of course, by the amounts of the individual current accounts, will represent the average velocity of circulation of deposit currency.   As in the case of coin and notes, payments made by way of loan or gift should, in theory, be excluded.

Let us now proceed to consider the causes which affect V, the velocity of circulation of coin.   This velocity, as has been pointed out, is measured by dividing the annual cash expenditure by the average amount of pocket-money.   Where cheques are not used, a change in the annual cash expenditure will usually cause a corresponding change in the average amount of pocket-money kept, and the ratio between the two will remain unaltered.   But it may easily happen that the average amount of pocket-money kept may change whilst the annual cash expenditure remains unaltered, and in such case there will be a change in the velocity of circulation. Such a change may be brought about by a tendency to increased thrift or greater extravagance.   A thriftless workman, for instance, who is paid on Saturday night, may have spent his whole wage by Monday, whilst his more careful companion will certainly have something still in hand.   If we suppose the total wage to be 21 shillings, of which the thriftless man spends one-half on Saturday night and the rest on Sunday, his average balance throughout the week will be $\dfrac{10\frac{1}{2}+0+0+0+0+0+0}{7}$

or $\dfrac{3}{2}$. If the careful man have the same wages, and spend 3 shillings on Saturday night and 3 shillings on every subsequent day, his average balance will be $\dfrac{18+15+12+9+6+3+0}{7}$, or 9. In the first case, since the total expenditure is 21 and the average balance $\frac{3}{2}$, the velocity of circulation will be $21/\frac{3}{2}$, or 14; whilst in the second case it will be $21/9$, or $\frac{7}{3}$. Thrift, that is to say, tends to decrease the velocity of circulation, extravagance to increase it.

A second factor which affects the velocity of circulation is the method of wage payment. Where wages are paid daily, or even weekly, the recipient can afford to keep little or no balance, trusting always to be able to tide over the interval until next pay day. If, however, wages are paid at longer intervals he must keep a certain amount of money in hand to meet expenses during the latter part of each interval. But, the larger the average stock of pocket-money, the slower, other things being equal, will be the velocity of circulation. Neglecting the fact that the less frequent wage payments are often made by cheque, we may say, therefore, that the more frequently wages are paid the greater will be the velocity of circulation of coin. A third and very important factor which requires consideration here is the system of shop credit. Where all purchases have to be paid for in cash the would-be purchaser must keep by him a stock of ready money sufficient to meet every requirement. Where purchases can be put down to his account he may be able to dispense with almost the whole of this stock of coin. This fact is vividly presented to anyone who travels beyond the immediate neighbourhood of his home. At home, being known to all the traders, he can purchase nearly all he wants on credit, settling his account at such times as are convenient; and he need carry only such money as is necessary for an occasional tip. Outside these charmed limits, however, he must pay for everything with cash, and, accordingly, his pockets are heavy with unaccustomed sovereigns, or vocal with £5 notes. The necessity for carrying such a large balance of pocket-money will, of course, reduce the velocity of circulation, whilst an extension of shop credit will obviate the necessity for carrying much pocket-money and so will increase the velocity of circulation. Again, the velocity of circulation will be increased by closer settlement or, by what comes to the same thing, increased facilities of communication. If we imagine the round of circulation of coin to be from the worker to the shop, and back

again from the shop to the worker, the time taken
to complete this round will obviously be shortened
if the worker lives close to the shop. Just as in a
populous town the turn-over of goods relatively to
the stock kept is much larger than it would be in
a scattered village, so with the stock of coin also.
The effect of close settlement and of shop credit in
increasing the velocity of circulation of coin should
be distinguished, however, from their much more
important effect, described in the last chapter, of
encouraging the cheque habit.

Up to this point we have been considering the
velocity of circulation of coin and notes only, but
the circulation of deposit currency is subject to
some of the same influences. Close settlement and
rapidity of communication, whether by railway,
post, telegraph or telephone, affect both coin and
deposit currency in the same way. There is one
cause, however, which is more potent in affecting
deposit currency than in affecting coin. This
cause is a temporary one, viz., rising prices. When
prices are rising, merchants and manufactures,
anxious to benefit by the rise, spend all their available resources on goods and raw material, and,
when these are sold, immediately spend the pro-
ceeds on buying more. This will cause a rapid
turn-over of deposit currency, and probably an
increase in the velocity of circulation of coin also.

But since, at such periods, there is always a considerable amount of speculation which entails a demand for cheques but not for cash, the effect upon deposit currency will be greater than the effect upon cash.   It is found, in fact, by statistical investigations, that the rate of turn-over of bank deposits is greatest at the summit of a boom, and smallest in years of reaction.

We have now to deal with the methods of determining the velocities of circulation, both of coin and of deposit currency.   First, then, as to the velocity of circulation of coin.   The measurement of this velocity used to be considered as an insoluble problem, but it has lately been attacked with considerable success by several different methods.   The simplest and most direct method is exemplified by an investigation conducted at Yale University by Professor Irving Fisher.   " The plan was adopted of asking volunteers to keep an exact account for one month of the daily cash expenditures and balances at the beginning and end of each day.   It was found from these statistics that, for the 113 individuals who contributed these new data, the average annual rate of expenditure was $660, and the average cash on hand was almost exactly $10, giving the quotient 66 times a year. We may place the general average at 60.   We find a distinct relation between amount of expenditure and rate of turn-over within each group, thus :—

	Number of Cases.	Average Annual Rate of Expenditure.	Average Cash Balance.	Velocity of Circulation.
Expending less than $600 a year	72	$367	$8·60	43
Expending $600 and over a year	41	1175	12·70	93

" Here we see that the richer men averaged about three times as great an expenditure as the poorer, but carried only 50 *per cent.* more cash in hand. . . . The progressive relation between expenditure and rate of turn-over may be seen by arranging the 113 cases into five groups according to expenditure :—

	Number of Cases.	Average Expenditure.	Velocity of Circulation.
Expending less than $300 a year	22	179	17
Expending over $300 and under $600	50	450	59
Expending over $600 and under $900	19	781	61
Expending over $900 and under $1200	10	1012	96
Expending over $1200 a year .	12	1936	137

We conclude, therefore, with at least a moderate degree of confidence, that, for a given price level, the greater the expenditure the higher the rate of turn-over." [1]

The figure of 60 adopted by Professor Irving Fisher as the average rate of turn-over amongst Yale students is much too high to be applied to the country as a whole. Amongst other reasons for this we may point to the facts that such students are a fairly well-to-do body, living in a busy town, and mostly keeping banking accounts. A more representative figure will emerge from the second and more exhaustive method, also due to Professor Irving Fisher. This method is based upon the generalization that the community may be divided into three classes : (1) a class consisting roughly of so-called " professional men," the members of which keep private banking accounts ; (2) a class composed of " commercial men," the members of which keep business banking accounts ; and (3) a class of wage-earners who keep no banking accounts. The cash transactions of the community may also be divided under three heads : (1) where members of the professional or commercial classes draw money from the bank and use it in purchasing goods ; (2) where the members of these two classes draw money from the bank and use it in paying

[1] *The Purchasing Power of Money*, pp. 380-382.

wages ; and (3) where wage-earners use their wages in cash payment for goods. These transactions will include practically all the cash transactions of the community. All others will be effected by cheque. How, then, are we to find out the total of these cash transactions ? It has been already pointed out that, as a general rule, money drawn out from a bank to be used for the purchase of *goods* performs only one exchange before it again re-enters a bank. Therefore the total amount of cash exchanges under head (1) will simply be equal to the amount of cash withdrawn from the bank during the period in question, *for the purpose of purchasing goods*. The total of cash exchanges under head (2), *i.e.* the total amount of cash exchanged against services, will obviously be equal to the amount of cash drawn out during this period for the purpose of paying wages. This amount, together with the amount under head (1), will, then, be simply the total amount of cash drawn from the banks, *for any purpose*, during the given period. Finally, the total of cash transactions under head (3) will be roughly equivalent to the total amount of wages paid in cash during this period. With the aid of statistics, not available in the case of England, Professor Irving Fisher has estimated the total amount of cash withdrawn from the United States banks in 1909 as 20·7 billions of dollars, whilst the total cash wages were 13·1 billions. Adding 1·3 billions for other exchanges (for which see Appendix C) he arrives at a total of cash transactions of 35·1 billions. The total circulation of notes and coin being estimated at 1·63 billions, we get :—

Total cash exchanges =MV=35·1 billions.
Total cash currency   =M = 1·63 billions.
Velocity of circulation=V   =21·5.

It will be noticed that this figure differs considerably from that obtained for the circulation of cash amongst Yale students.

Up to the present we have described the two more important methods of measuring the velocity of coin. Now we may pass to a somewhat simpler problem—the measurement of the velocity of circulation of deposit currency. It is easy to see that if the average total of current accounts over a given period is £M', and the total of cheques drawn during that period is £X, then the average velocity of circulation is X/M'. The difficulty of the problem lies in measuring the quantities M' and X. In several continental countries, however, the necessary figures are available, and M. Pierre des Essars, using the formula V'=X/M', has worked out over a long period of years the rate of turn-over of deposit currency for several large banks, whilst Professor Irving Fisher has applied the same

F

formula to the case of the United States as a whole. The figures thus obtained are interesting, inasmuch as they give a clear illustration of two important facts which have been anticipated on theoretical grounds. First, that the rate of turn-over is greatest in panic years, or in the years immediately preceding them. Second, that the velocity of circulation varies directly with the density of population. Thus the rate of turn-over for Berlin is 150, as compared with 110 in Paris and Brussels, 40 in Rome, 30 in Lisbon, and 15 in Madrid. For the United States as a whole the average rapidity of circulation was 36 in 1896 and 50 in 1911. For England as a whole the calculations of the author indicate 34 as an approximate figure. This figure, however, must be accepted with some reserve, for, in the case of England, we have neither the periodical returns available in the case of Continental banks, nor the results of elaborate investigations such as those upon which are based the calculations of Professors Kemmerer and Fisher.

CHAPTER VI

Now let us return once more to the equations which we have considered at such length. In Chapter IV. it has been shown that, where M is the amount of money and M′ the amount of deposit currency in circulation, V and V′ their respective velocities of circulation, R the volume of trade, and P the level of prices,

$$MV + M'V' = RP.$$

It now remains to consider which of the six quantities comprised in this equation vary independently of the other terms, and which do not vary independently. The importance of this inquiry may be seen by looking at the end which we have in view. This end is to prove that the magnitude of P is dependent upon the magnitudes of the other terms of the equation, and will not vary independently of them, viz., that the level of prices varies with, *and in consequence of*, changes in, *e.g.* the velocity of circulation of money, or of the amount of the deposit currency. As the equation stands it might be equally true that P was an independent variable, and that the velocity of circulation of money or the amount of deposit currency varied with, and in consequence of changes in the level of prices. And this would be a very different thing. Let us then take each term separately, and see whether changes in that term are independent of changes in other terms.

To begin with R, the volume of trade. This quantity is obtained by multiplying the number of units produced in a given time by the average number of times which each unit changes hands in that time, and is clearly an independent variable, if we neglect mere temporary fluctuations. The quantity of goods produced in a year depends, broadly speaking, upon the productive capacity of the community, and will only be temporarily and slightly altered by rising or falling prices, whilst the average number of times which each unit changes hands, though it may be temporarily increased by the speculation consequent upon rising prices, depends normally upon the state of business organization. We may say, therefore, that in the long run R is independent of P. It is clearly independent, also, of changes in M, M', V and V'.

Next as to V and V', the velocities of circulation of money and of deposit currency. We have already given an account of the forces which affect these quantities, and by referring to that account it will be seen that changes in business habits were the chief of these forces. Changes in the quantity of money or of deposit currency in circulation will have no marked effects upon business habits, and will not affect the velocities of circulation. It may well be, however, that an increase in R, the volume of trade, leading to closer settlement and to an increase of banking facilities, will cause both V and V′ to increase. Changes in P, the level of prices, it is important to note, cannot affect V or V′ except temporarily in years of trade excitement or depression.

Next as to M′, the amount of deposit currency. The quantity M′V′, as has already been pointed out, bears a fairly constant ratio to the quantity MV, so long as other things remain the same. If, then, we assume V and V′ to be constant, we may conclude that M′, the amount of deposit currency, will vary directly with M, the amount of cash in circulation. It is true that the ratio of M′ to M may be affected by an increase of R, the volume of trade, leading to an extension of banking facilities ; but in so far as changes in P only are concerned, we may say that M′ is a constant multiple of M. But since, as will be seen subsequently, the quantity M is not influenced by changes in the quantity P, there is no ground for stating that M′ will be influenced by P, the level of prices.

So far, then, we have seen that, except for purely temporary effects, R, V and V' are independent of P, whilst M' is influenced *directly* only by M and R. It remains to be seen whether M, and consequently M', is independent of P. It will be remembered that we have already given a proof of the purely algebraic relation,

$$MV + M'V' = RP.$$

Now, assuming the validity of this equation, if R, V and V' remain unchanged, an increase of P must be accompanied by a corresponding change of M, and consequently of M'. Let us assume that it is the change in P which causes the changes of M and M', *i.e.* that a rise of prices causes an increase in the amount of coin and deposit currency in circulation. In such a case where are we to get the gold thus to increase the circulation and to act as reserve for the increase of deposits ? In these days of organized banking there are practically no unused hoards of gold waiting for a demand for coinage. The only sources of supply are the mines and the gold in use in the arts. But gold cannot be obtained at a moment's notice from the mines, so we are compelled to turn for our supplies to gold used in or destined for use in the arts. Now we have already assumed a rise of prices, that is, a rise of prices of " all other goods," for the price of gold

ornaments cannot vary either upwards or down-
wards. But if the prices of " all other goods "
rise, whilst the price of gold ornaments remains
stationary, this will cause people to buy more gold
ornaments than they did formerly. Thus the
assumption that a rise in the level of prices may
(apart from temporary fluctuations) *cause* an increase in the amount of coin in circulation leads
us to these two contradictory conclusions : (1)
that the increased amount of coin will be taken,
in part at any rate, from gold used in the arts ; and
(2) that the amount of gold used in the arts will
increase. We may therefore conclude that the
assumption from which follows this absurd result
is wrong, and that changes in the amount of coin
in circulation are not caused by changes in the level
of prices. But, since there *is* a causal relation
between these two quantities, it follows necessarily
from this conclusion that changes in price are
caused by changes in the amount of coin in circulation. Hence we see that in the equation

$$MV + M'V' = RP,$$

the factor P is (except in cases of merely temporary
fluctuations) a dependent variable ; that is, it
depends for its magnitude upon the other terms of
the equation, and has no effect upon their magnitudes.

Here we have, in its modern form, the famous "quantity theory" of money, which shows us that the level of prices depends upon the volume of trade, the quantity of currency and of deposit currency in circulation, and on their respective velocities of circulation. This theory has been adopted by almost every economist of repute, both ancient and modern. It has, however, been ably attacked by a few ardent spirits who prefer to pin their faith to the so-called "cost of production" theory.

According to the cost of production theory the general level of prices is determined by the cost of production of goods as compared with the cost of production of gold, and the level of prices so determined fixes the amount of coin required for circulation. A rise or fall in the level of prices will, other things being equal, cause an increase or decrease of the coin in circulation ; just the opposite to the sequence of cause and effect postulated by the quantity theory.

It is admitted by partisans of the cost of production theory that, the stock of gold in existence being so large and so durable, changes in the cost of production *of gold* can only effect secular changes in the level of prices. "Changes in price due to events influencing gold itself (and not arising from goods) must in the very nature of things be ex-

tremely slow and gradual in their operation." [1]
Suppose, for instance, that at any given time the
quantity of gold in circulation be represented by
1000, its velocity of circulation by 20, the volume
of trade by 2000, and the annual production of
gold by 1. Then, omitting considerations of deposit
currency, since

$$MV = RP$$

the level of prices, P, must be 10. Then, if by an
invention the cost of production of gold be so
cheapened as to enable new mines to keep up a
production of 19 units of gold annually until such
time as the price level had doubled,[2] the annual
production of gold will be 20 units. If we suppose
all gold produced to be added to the currency, and
if all other factors, such as the volume of trade,
etc., remain unchanged, the amount of coin in
circulation, and therefore the price level, will
double in 1000/20, or 50 years. By the end of 50
years, that is to say, the price level will have risen
to correspond with the decreased cost of production of gold. But it is obvious that forces which
take 50 years or even 30 years to adjust themselves will never come to equilibrium except by
accident. Long before equilibrium has been

---

[1] *The Principles of Money*, Laughlin, p. 337.

[2] That is, we assume the cost of production of gold to be halved.

attained other changes will come about, which may throw the point of equilibrium in quite another place. When the forces begin to adjust themselves to these new conditions another change may take place, and so on for ever. Of course no one will deny that the value of gold *tends* to approximate to its cost of production. This is quite true. But it is also true that the tendency never, except by accident, comes anywhere near fulfilment. This is admitted both by the quantity and by the cost of production schools. In regard, however, to the effect of the cost of production of goods we find them at issue. To illustrate their difference let us consider seven commodities, A, B, C, D, E, F and G, of which G represents gold, and the other letters any six other commodities. Both schools will admit, of course, that if the expenses of production of commodity A be decreased, the price of A will fall. To this the cost of production school, as represented by Professor Laughlin, will add that the level of prices is made up from the actual quotations of single articles, and that hence " the forces affecting the level of prices are the same as those affecting the prices of single commodities which enter into the resultant." [1] Therefore, if the expenses of production of one or more of commodities A, B, C, D, E, and F are lowered, the

[1] *The Principles of Money*, p. 353.

general level of prices will be lowered also. The general level of prices, that is to say, " supposing that the agencies directly touching gold are constant, is governed by the high or low expenses of production of goods." [1]   The quantity school, on the other hand, do not admit the analogy between general and particular prices. According to them an improvement in the production of one article may lower the price *of that article*, but neither an improvement in the production of one article nor an improvement in the production of all articles will, other things remaining the same, alter the general level of prices. Given a pint of water and six cylindrical vases the level of water in any one vase may be altered by taking water to or from other vases, but no amount of rearrangement will alter the average level of water in the vases. Nothing will alter that but a change in the total quantity of the water or in the total capacity of the vases. No matter how much the processes of production be improved, there will be no general fall of prices unless the volume of trade expands more rapidly than the volume of currency ; account being taken also of the velocity of circulation.

To consider the matter from another point of view let us take a factor to which has often been ascribed a general rise of prices, *i.e.* the rise of

[1] *The Principles of Money*, p. 355.

wages consequent upon the organization of labour.
According to Professor Laughlin such a general rise
of wages must cause a general rise of prices, *because
it implies greater expenses of production.* According to the quantity theory the sequence of cause
and effect will be quite different. Let us suppose
that by a general strike the working men of a country
had obtained a rise in wages of 10 *per cent.* all round.
Owing to larger wage-bills industry would become
less profitable, and the less stable businesses would
close. In consequence of this, production would
diminish and the volume of trade would decrease.
This decrease in the volume of trade, and not the
rise in expenses of production, would then cause a
rise of prices. To this analysis, however, it may
be objected that the producers would raise their
prices immediately the concession of higher wages
had been made, and before any contraction of
trade had taken place.

This may be true, but it is equally true that such
a rise of prices could not be maintained unless
followed by a contraction of trade. If the volume
of production continued as before, and if demand
also continued as before (and there is no reason
why demand should change), how could prices
alter ? The rise of prices would, under the stress
of competition, inevitably fall again to its previous
level, the weaker businesses would fail, the volume

of trade would diminish, and then, and then only, would there be a permanent rise in the general level of prices.   A general rise of wages, then, will cause a general rise of prices, not because it implies greater expenses of production, but because it implies a decrease in the volume of trade.   If, owing to some temporary cause, such as a good harvest or a burst of speculation, a general rise of wages were not followed by a decrease in the volume of trade, the general level of prices, other things remaining the same, would not rise.

CHAPTER VII

IN previous chapters we have talked of the " level of prices," but have made no attempt to show how we may measure the changes of this level of prices, or of its converse, the purchasing power of money. The problem, indeed, is a somewhat intricate one owing to the mass of material to be dealt with. We have to consider a vast number of commodities, some of which may be falling in price, others rising, and others remaining stationary, and from this conflicting maze of figures we have to disentangle the general trend of prices. The method by which this is done is known as the method of index-numbers, and may be shortly described as follows :—Take a limited number of the more important commodities, find out the prices of these commodities at regular intervals over the period to be considered, and, by combining these figures, find out the average movement of prices over the required period. In this method, however, there are two main difficulties. First, what commodities are we to select ? Second, how are we to combine together the prices of these commodities when ascertained ? It is obvious, in the first place, that a poor man will take no interest in the price of broughams or of race-horses. He will be vitally affected by the price of bread and clothes, but he will be entirely indifferent to the price of expensive luxuries. In fact, to find out the effect of changing prices upon different classes, we require entirely different index-numbers, each constructed on the basis of the principal articles of consumption of the class concerned. An index-number for the labouring class could be constructed from the prices of a few necessaries comprised under the heads, rent, food, drink, and clothing, whilst an index-number for the wealthier classes would require a more elaborate list. To mention one important item only ; the wages of labour would seem a necessary part of the expenses of the rich, whilst it would find no place in the budget of a navvy. Another type of commodity which would be used for the index-number of the rich only is machinery and " producer's goods " generally. The working man, for all practical purposes, may be said to spend his money on consumer's goods only. All that he buys will be for immediate use or consumption. The rich man, after having spent part of his income on consumer's goods, may still have something over for investment, and the price of steel, timber, and other producer's goods will therefore be of interest to him. Still it is questionable, even in the case of the rich, whether producer's goods should not be excluded from their index-number. Money spent on consumer's goods is spent almost entirely in the native country of the spender, whilst his investments may be made in different countries, and at varying price levels. To include producer's goods at " world prices " in the list of commodities would therefore lead to the formation of an index-number so complicated that it could hardly be advocated in practice.

So far we have talked of index-numbers for special sections of the community. The best known index-numbers, however, are designed to represent changes in the level of prices as they affect a whole country. The articles selected as these bases of such index-numbers are usually the principal imports and exports of the country concerned. Whatever the purpose of the index-number, however, the articles chosen as its bases should be such that their identity remains the same over the period of years considered. To take a simple example ; it would be of little use comparing the price of cloth in 1912 with the price of cloth in 1812, because the two cloths would be of very different quality. Again, the price of a sheep in 1912 should not be compared with the price of a sheep in 1312, without taking account of the much greater weight and wool-bearing capacity of the modern animal. Other articles again disappear altogether with the lapse of time, and other entirely new ones come into existence. It would be useless, for instance, when comparing the prices of 1912 with those of 1812, to include such things as beaver hats or motor-cars. All these considerations tend to restrict the number of commodities available for the preparation of index-numbers.

We have now to turn to our second difficulty. Given the commodities with which we are to work, how shall the prices of these be combined so as to form an index-number ? In order to illustrate some of the combinations which have been adopted, I propose to construct various index-numbers from the prices of five articles, viz., a bushel of wheat, a horse, a sheep, a pound of butter, and a gallon of beer, for the years 1550, 1675 and 1795. I must point out, however, that index-numbers calculated from these data can be of little use except for purposes of illustration. In the first place the number of articles is much too small. In the second place, as we have already pointed out, the modern sheep is really quite a different article to its mediæval representative. Similarly with regard to horses, and possibly with regard to beer also. Returning, however, to our index-numbers, let us consider Columns I., II. and III. of Table I. Here are set down in pence the prices of the five articles for the

G

TABLE I.

Column	I.	II.	III.	IV.	V.	VI.	VII.	VIII.	IX.	Line.
Year	1550	1675	1795	1550	1675	1795	1550	1675	1795	1
Bushel of Wheat	34	54	94	100	158	277	63	100	174	2
Horse	504	1320	4560	100	262	905	39	100	345	3
Sheep	52	132	456	100	254	877	39	100	345	4
Pound of Butter	5	4	11	100	80	220	125	100	275	5
Gallon of Beer	2	8	5	100	400	250	25	100	62	6
Totals	597	1518	5126	500	1154	2529	291	500	1201	7
Bradstreet's Index-No.	100	271	859	...	...	...	...	...	...	8
Arithmetic Mean	...	...	...	Base 100	year 231	1550 506	Base 58	year 100	1675 240	9
Arith. Mean, Different Base	...	...	...	Base 100	year 173	1675 401	Base 43	year 100	1550 219	10
Weighted, Arith. Mean	...	...	...	100	161	328	...	...	...	11
Geometric Mean	...	...	...	Base 100	year 202	1550 413	Base 49	year 100	1675 204	12
Geom. Mean, Different Base	...	...	...	Base 100	year 204	1675 416	Base 49	year 100	1550 204	13

years under consideration. In line 7, at the bottom of each column, are the totals of the respective columns, showing the total price in pence for each year, of one bushel of wheat, together with one horse, one sheep, one pound of butter, and one gallon of beer. In line 8 are these totals so reduced that the total for the base year (1550) is 100. The figures so obtained might be used as index-numbers. We might say, that is, that the index-numbers for 1675 and 1795 are 271 and 859 respectively. And an index-number obtained by this method has, in fact, been used in America under the name of Bradstreet's Index-number. It is, of course, very simple to calculate, but has this great disadvantage that it gives an undue influence to changes in the prices of the relatively expensive articles. In our example, for instance, the most expensive article is a horse, and the great rise in the price of horses which took place between 1550 and 1795 has, therefore, had an unduly large influence, and has so caused the index-number for 1795 to be unduly high.

Going on now to Column IV. of the Table, we find here that the prices of all articles for 1550 have been equated to 100. In Columns V. and VI. are figures so calculated that they bear to 100 the same relation as do the prices in Columns II. and III. to the prices in Column I., *e.g.* $100/158 = 34/54$, $100/277 =$

34/94, and so on. In fact, the figures in Columns
V. and VI. are really price-ratios, not prices.[1]   In
line 7 are the totals of Columns IV., V. and VI., and
in line 9 are these totals so reduced that the figure
of the base year (1550) is 100. Thus the figures in
line 9 corresponding to the years 1675 and 1795 are
the arithmetic means of the ratios of prices for
those years. The arithmetic means thus obtained
are often used as index-numbers. As in this
method the number for the base year is the same
—100—for each article, it is obvious that the
arithmetic mean is not subject to the main defect
of Bradstreet's Index-number. But there is
another defect of a somewhat subtle nature to
which the arithmetic mean *is* liable. If, for instance, the price of any commodity, x, in the base
year is $_1P_x$, the price-ratio for this commodity in
the year n will be $_nP_x/_1P_x$, and in the year $n+1$ will
be $_{n+1}P_x/_1P_x$. From these formulæ we see that, if
in the base year the price of x is abnormally high,
the variations in the price-ratios of x for subsequent
years will be unfairly minimized as compared with
the variations in price-ratios of other articles of which

[1] If we represent the price of article x in year n by $_nP_x$, then the
price-ratios will be represented by formulas such as $\frac{_2P_1}{_1P_1} \times 100$, or
$\frac{_3P_2}{_1P_2} \times 100$

the price was not unduly high in the base year. From this follow two conclusions :—First, that the arithmetic mean will vary according as different years are chosen as base. Second, that if the arithmetic mean be adopted as an index-number it will be well to choose as a base year one in which the articles concerned sold for normal prices. In order to illustrate the first conclusion I have set out in Columns VII., VIII. and IX. the price-ratios for the same years and for the same articles, but taking as the base year 1675 instead of 1550. This variation of the arithmetic mean of price-ratios according to the year taken as base is a distinct disadvantage, but on the whole this mean forms a reliable index-number, and is largely used.

A variety of the simple arithmetic mean is the " weighted " mean. It is obvious, when looking at the course of prices from the point of view of an individual consumer, that a change in the price of bread or of milk is more important than a change in the price of salt or of pepper. The more of a thing a man uses the more important to him are changes of its price. On this principle it is often the custom in making index-numbers to give greater weight to the price-ratios of those commodities which are most largely consumed. The process of weighting may be explained as follows :—The simple arithmetic mean of, *e.g.* the price-ratios in Column V., is obtained by dividing the sum of the ratios by their number, thus—

$$\frac{158+262+254+80+400}{5}=231.$$

But, supposing we wish to weight the more important articles, we must, instead of writing down the price-ratio of the weighted article once, write it down as many times as we wish to weight it. Thus, if we wish to give a weight of 10 to wheat and 5 to butter, whilst the other articles are weighted by unity, the weighted mean of the price-ratios in Column V. becomes

$$\frac{158\times10+262+254+80\times5+400}{18}=161.$$

The divisor has become 18 because we have 10 of the 158 ratio, 5 of the 80 ratio, and 3 others. The number of ratios has therefore become $10+5+3$, or 18. When using a small number of articles upon which to base an index-number weighting is essential, for in such cases one or two important commodities may be entirely swamped by large price movements in an opposite sense of the less important commodities. But if the number of articles chosen be large and includes many important commodities, it is highly probable that the variations of the prices of these important commodities will, in general, correspond with the variations of prices of the less important commodities, and weighting will not be needed. If there is any connection, however, between the importance of the commodities and the extent or direction of changes in their price, weighting will be necessary, however large the number of articles chosen.

Another form of index-number which requires attention is the geometric mean. This is obtained by multiplying the necessary price-ratios together and taking of the product a root equal to the number of ratios. The geometric mean of the price-ratios in Column V., for instance, is

$$\sqrt[5]{158 \times 262 \times 254 \times 80 \times 400} = 202.$$

This index-number has several merits. It does not give undue prominence to exceptionally high numbers, and it is independent of the choice of base year. It may be easily seen, for instance, that the index-numbers obtained by this method from Columns IV., V. and VI. are equivalent to those obtained from the figures of Columns VII., VIII. and IX., though the base years are different. In spite of these virtues, however, the geometric mean seems to have fallen into disfavour of recent years. Its place in popularity is being taken by the *median*, the simplest of all index-numbers. To obtain the median we take the price-ratios of the year under consideration, place them in order of magnitude, and select the middle ratio or, if the number of ratios be even, the arithmetic or geometric mean between the two middle ratios. The magnitude so obtained is the Median. In Column V., for instance, we have the following ratios : 80, 158, 254, 262, 400. The median of these is 254. As a matter of practice, where five ratios only are available the median would be quite unsuitable as an index-number, but where the number of articles treated is large the median is both simple and accurate. It is not affected, to the same extent as the arithmetic mean, by changes of the base year, and is not influenced by the occurrence of abnormally large or abnormally small price-ratios.

After this short description of the methods of measuring changes of the level of prices, let us proceed to discuss the various devices which have been suggested for avoiding such changes. Practically all the engagements of modern commerce are based upon the assumption that the purchasing power of money will remain unchanged, and it may be assumed without further discussion that great or sudden changes in this purchasing power are to be avoided if possible. The problem thus raised has elicited a number of suggestions of considerable interest and importance, of which a few may be described here.

First, then, as to the tabular standard.   The
theory of the tabular standard is based upon the
idea that if, in pursuance of a contract between
A and B, A agrees with B to pay £100 at some
future date, and if, at that date, £100 will buy more
or less than it does now, the agreement will be so
far nullified.   In the first case, B gets more than he
expected ; in the second case, less.   Might it not
be possible to avoid this evil by settling contracts
for future payments not in units of coin, but in units
of purchasing power ?   Let us take, for instance,
the unit as being such an amount of money as
would purchase 1 quarter of wheat, 1 ton of coal,
10 pounds of steel, and 1 pound of wool, and let us
suppose the total price of these goods in 1912 to be
£10.   Then, if the contract made in 1912 be for the
payment of £100 in 1920, it might be expressed in
terms of the tabular standard as being for the payment of 10 units of purchasing power in 1920.   If
by 1920 the purchasing power of money had halved,
i.e. if the total price of the articles enumerated in
the table had doubled, the payment of 10 units
would involve the payment in cash not of £100, but
of £200.   If, on the other hand, the purchasing
power of money had doubled, *i.e.* if the total price
of the specified articles had halved, the payment of
10 units of purchasing power would involve a cash
payment of only £50.   It has been suggested that

the State should undertake the publication of an index-number for use as a tabular standard, and should allow its use to be optional in all contracts. There is no doubt that in the case of contracts for annuities, pensions, and all other payments extending over long periods the use of such a standard might be very beneficial. Up to the present, it is true, the tabular standard has not been practically tested except where the " table " contained one commodity only, viz., corn. " We are forced to admit," said the late Professor Jevons in this connection, " that the statesmen of Queen Elizabeth were far-seeing when they passed the Act which obliged the colleges of Oxford, Cambridge, and Eton to lease their lands for corn rents. The result has been to make those colleges far richer than they would otherwise have been, the rents and endowments expressed in money having sunk to a fraction of their ancient value." It is to such long contracts that the use and the benefit of the tabular standard is likely to be confined. For the everyday transactions of modern commerce such an instrument would be unnecessarily troublesome, and is not likely to come into use.

Let us now turn to the subject of bimetallism, a subject which is now of not much practical value, but which, in addition to its historical importance, is of considerable theoretical interest. Put as shortly as possible the suggestion of the bimetallist is that the State should coin all the silver and gold offered at its mints, and should enact, in addition, that debts should be payable in either gold or silver, the equivalence of the two metals being fixed at (say) 16 to 1, so that a gold coin of any weight should be the monetary equivalent of 16 silver coins of equal weight. Under such circumstances any person possessing silver or gold could take it to the mint and obtain an equivalent of coin, and any debtor could pay his debts either in silver or gold. Thus, says the bimetallist, we would obtain two benefits ; first, that the values of silver and gold would be kept at a constant ratio, and that therefore the exchanges between gold-and-silver-standard countries would be saved from violent fluctuation ; second, that the general level of prices would be more steady. The monometallist maintains, on the other hand, that the values of gold and silver could not be kept at a constant ratio merely by legislative enactment, and that, even were it possible to maintain this ratio, this would not necessarily involve greater stability in the purchasing power of money. With regard to the question whether a constant ratio is maintainable the following argument seems conclusive : " Let us assume that gold and silver are coined freely by Government, and made legally current in unlimited

amount at a fixed rate ; and let us assume that this
rate in the first instance accurately corresponds to
the relative market values of the two metals as they
would exist apart from legal interference. Let us
then suppose that the supply of silver becomes
more abundant, the conditions determining the
values of all other products remaining unaltered.
Then, apart from legal interference, the gold price
of silver would fall ; but under the circumstances
supposed this cannot take place in the first instance, for no one will exchange his silver in the
market for a smaller amount of gold coin than he
could get by taking the silver to the mint to be
coined. Hence . . . all the additional supply of
silver, which the non-monetary demand will not
absorb at the legal rate, will go to the mint, the
purchasing power of the whole mass of coin will
fall correspondingly, gold and silver being maintained at their legal relative value. As the exchange
value of bullion relatively to other wares must, of
course, fall equally, an extension will take place in
the non-monetary demand for bullion—gold as well
as silver. But as no change is supposed to occur in
the conditions of supply of gold bullion there must
be a corresponding diminution in the gold sent to
the mint for coinage. If the increase in the supply
of silver were not very great or permanent, its
effects might stop at this point, so that no differ-

ence would manifest itself between the market rate
and the mint rate of interchange of the two metals ;
the demand having, in fact, under the pressure of
governmental interference, adjusted itself to the
supply. . . . But if the addition to annual supply
be sufficiently extensive and prolonged, the process
above described may be carried on until no gold at
all is sent to the mint ; and then for the first time,
if the process still goes on, the market price of gold
bullion will begin to rise.   When this rise has gone
so far that the gold coins still in use have actually
—through the continued depreciation of silver,
which necessarily drags down with it the value of
the coined gold as well—become less valuable than
the bullion which they on the average contain, it
will become profitable to melt them down ;   and,
if the same causes continue to operate, this process
will continue until the coin used in large payments
is entirely composed of the metal that has fallen
in value.   It thus appears that the adoption of a
double standard will prevent slight variations in
supply from affecting the relative market value of
the two metals.   But variations of a certain magnitude cannot be thus counteracted ;   on the contrary, such variations will nullify the formal adoption of a double standard and render the currency
practically monometallic.   If, now, we suppose the
country contemplated to be in commercial relations

with other countries in which the double standard is not adopted, the nullification of the double standard will be accelerated, since the non-monetary demand for gold in the country with the double standard will be partly a demand for exportation to other countries where the value of gold is not legislatively tied to that of silver." [1]

A very ingenious mechanism (see Fig. 2) to illustrate the various points involved in this problem has been devised by Professor Irving Fisher. Let A and C be the sections of two hollow vessels connected by a pipe P. In one side of the vessel A are several inlets I_1, I_2, I_3 . . . through which pour streams of liquid representing gold. In the other side of A and in both sides of C are outlets O_1, O_2, O_3 . . . through which this liquid may escape. The inlets I_1, I_2 . . . represent mines, the volume of liquid in A represents the stock of gold bullion, the volume of liquid in C represents gold coin, the outlets in A represent the consumption of gold for various industrial and artistic purposes, whilst the outlets in C represent wastage and loss of coin. The height of the liquid in C (which will be the same as in A) may be taken to represent the level of prices. [2] Those inlets into A which are

---

[1] *Principles of Economics*, H. Sidgwick, Bk. II. c. v.

[2] From considerations of space and of simplicity I have omitted

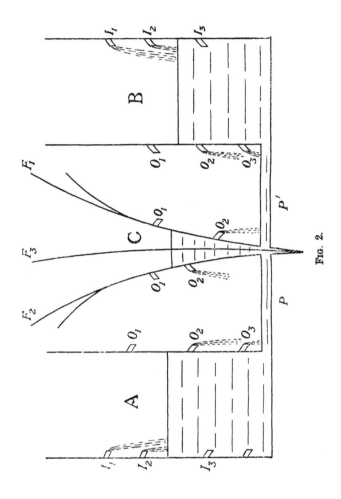

Fig. 2.

below the level of the liquid are assumed to be closed. The existence of inlets and outlets at different levels illustrates the fact that, as the level of prices falls (or as the value of gold rises), more mines will be worked, and less gold will be taken for the arts. *Vice versa*, as the level of prices rises (and as the value of gold falls correspondingly) the less productive mines will be closed, and more gold will be used for the arts. The mechanism as described up to this point represents a country having a gold currency and a free coinage of gold. Let us now proceed to consider the cylinder B. This cylinder with its inlets, its liquid contents, and its outlets represents silver mines, a stock of silver bullion, and the consumption of this bullion in industries and arts, whilst the height of the liquid in B represents the level of prices as measured in silver. Then let us suppose that the country under consideration proposes to adopt bimetallism, *i.e.* that it proposes to allow the free flow of silver from its silver bullion market B into its monetary vessel C. To represent accurately the effects which would ensue from such a change, we must draw the cylinder B on a scale corresponding to the bimetallic ratio to be adopted. For instance, if silver is going to be admitted on equal terms with gold, *i.e.* if a silver

any reference to Professor Fisher's elegant device for illustrating the marginal utility of gold.

coin weighing one ounce is to be declared by law
to be equal in value to a gold coin weighing one
ounce, the cylinder B and its contents must be
drawn on the same scale as the cylinder A and its
contents, so that a drop of water from either represents an equal weight of metal. If, however, the
more reasonable ratio of 1 to 16 is to be adopted,
and one gold coin of one ounce is going to be equivalent to sixteen silver coins of one ounce each, the
cylinder B and its contents must be drawn on one-
sixteenth the scale of cylinder A.[1]   Then if a drop of
water from B represents sixteen ounces of silver, an
equal drop of water from A will represent one ounce
of gold.   Keeping this complication in mind we can
now see from the model in what way the country
under consideration would be affected by the adoption of bimetallism.   Let us suppose that inside
the vessel C there is a flexible film F which can be
driven from one side of C to the other according to
the variations of pressure, and which will keep the
liquids coming from A and B from mixing in C.
Before the pipe P' is opened this film will be at F_1.
When the pipe P' is opened, i.e. when bimetallism
is adopted, three things may happen. First, the
height and volume of the liquid in B may be such

[1] This does not of course mean that B will be smaller than A, for
the stock of silver may well be more than sixteen times as large as
the stock of gold.

H

as to push the film F right across C to a position F_2, so that all the gold liquid is forced back into the bullion market, A, and the vessel C becomes full of silver liquid. That is to say, if silver is valued too highly, the adoption of bimetallism will result in the melting down of all gold coin and the establishment of silver monometallism. Second, the height and volume of the liquid in B may be such that the opening of P has no effect upon the film F, and C remains full of gold liquid. Here the undervaluing of silver has resulted in the continuance of gold monometallism. Third, there is the intermediate possibility that the film may be pushed to a position F_3, and the vessel C filled partly with gold and partly with silver fluid. Here, temporarily at least, bimetallism has been established, though it is obvious that the position thus attained may easily be imperilled by changes in the supply either of gold or silver. It should be noticed that the chances of a bimetallic scheme being successful will be greatest (1) where at the moment of adoption the level of liquid in B is the same as in A, *i.e.* where the legal bimetallic ratio corresponds to the market ratio, and (2) where the volume of C is great as compared with the volumes of B and A, *i.e.* where the monetary demand is great as compared with the non-monetary demand. This second condition is obviously fulfilled in the case of international bimetallism, where bimetallism at a given ratio is adopted by agreement between a number of countries.

Now let us turn to our second question—whether the level of prices would be steadier under a bimetallic than under a monometallic régime ? Obviously changes of price level due to alterations in the volume of trade or in the velocity of circulation of money would continue to the same extent under either system. It would only be changes in price level due to alterations in the supply of money-material that could be affected. Now it is obvious that, in all probability, the total supply of gold and silver would be more constant in amount than the supply of one only of those metals. It is possible, on the other hand, that if the supply of (say) silver be much more irregular than the supply of gold, a monetary system based on gold and silver would be more unstable than one based on gold only. " Two variable metals joined through bimetallism may be likened to two tipsy men locking arms. Together they may walk somewhat more steadily than apart although, if one happens to be much more sober than the other, his own gait may be made worse by the union."

Symmetallism, the monetary theory associated with the name of Professor Marshall, is a modification of Ricardo's *Proposals for an Economic and*

Secure Currency.   Ricardo suggested that the State should continue to issue token coins of silver and bronze, but, instead of minting gold coins, should issue notes in exchange for gold *bars*, and should give gold bars in exchange for notes ; these notes to be the only legal tender.   Professor Marshall proposed to use bars not of gold only, but of silver and gold both.   " A gold bar of 100 grammes, together with a silver bar, say, 20 times as heavy, would be exchangeable at the Issue Department for an amount of [notes] which would be calculated and fixed once for all when the scheme was introduced.   If we wished the value of the currency to be regulated chiefly by gold we should have only a small bar of silver ; if chiefly by silver we should have, perhaps, fifty or one hundred times as heavy a bar of silver as that of gold." [1]   As compared with bimetallism, the chief point to notice about Professor Marshall's plan is that it involves no fixed ratio between the prices of gold and silver, and presents no danger of breaking down.   " If adopted by several nations it would constitute at once a perfect international basis of currency and prices.   France could, if it chose, still reckon in francs, England in pounds, and America in dollars ; but every 20 franc note [and every pound and 5 dollar note] would state on its face how many

[1] Gold and Silver Commission.   Evidence Q. 9837.

francs [pounds or dollars] were exchangeable for a standard pair of bars. . . . Francs, pounds, and dollars would alike give a definite command over bars of gold and silver which would form a perfect medium for international payments." [1] As regards the steadying of prices it should be noticed that under bimetallism, where the ratio of the two metals is fixed, an increase or decrease in the cost of production of either metal will give a violent impetus to a corresponding decrease or increase of production of that metal, whereas under symmetallism, where the ratio of the two metals is not fixed, the impetus so given to changes of production will not be nearly so great. Hence we may expect prices to. be steadier under symmetallism than under bimetallism.

Another scheme—that of a "tabular currency" —for steadying prices resembles those of Ricardo and of Professor Marshall in that, under it, the monetary system of the State is to consist of metal token coins of small value and of paper legal tender. This paper represents so many units of purchasing power, according to a tabular standard, and is to be redeemable in gold, the amount of gold so given varying with changes in the level of prices. Suppose, for instance, that when such a scheme was started the level of prices was represented by

[1] Gold and Silver Commission.   Evidence, Q. 9837.

100, and a unit of paper currency was made exchangeable for an ounce of gold. So long as no change was made an ounce of gold, being freely exchangeable for paper currency, would perforce retain the same price when expressed in terms of such currency. But if, on December 31st, at the end of the year, it is announced by the Statistical Office, which would have to be established under this scheme, that the level of prices has risen to 110, the gold equivalent of the paper currency will also be raised by one-tenth. Then every person holding a paper unit will be able to get one-tenth more gold on January 1st than he could on December 31st ; though, as regards goods other than gold, he will be able to buy no more on the former date than on the latter. That is, the price of gold will fall by one-eleventh, and will remain fixed at that lower level, whilst the price of other goods will, temporarily at any rate, remain the same. But the relative *utilities* of gold and of other goods will not have been altered, and therefore traders will buy gold in preference to other goods until the relative *prices* return to their former level. That is to say, notes will be returned, and gold demanded until, through the ensuing restriction of the currency, the price level of commodities other than gold has fallen by one - eleventh — practically to its former level. By thus adjusting the currency from time to time a stable level of prices could be assured.

A scheme designed with the sole object of steadying prices is the *billon regulateur* of M. Leon Walras. M. Walras suggested that the gold-standard States, whilst maintaining the free coinage of gold, should issue silver token coins as a subsidiary legal tender. A commission designed to ascertain changes in the general price level should then control the issue of these tokens to such amounts as would keep the purchasing power of money as constant as possible. The issue of token coins, of course, implies a profit to the State, but such profits would have to be set aside to provide against the equivalent expense of withdrawing coin if a contraction of the currency were indicated. It may be well imagined, however, that if highly productive gold mines were discovered, the currency might become so enlarged that a withdrawal even of the whole of the token silver would not prevent a great rise of prices. The prospect of such an eventuality leads naturally to the idea that a congress of States capable of establishing a *billon regulateur* might with equal ease put a stop to the free coinage of gold, and conform their issues of gold coin to the advice of a monetary commission. Such an idea certainly has the merit of simplicity and directness. Of course, if the output of gold from the mines became very great, and only a small portion of this output were minted, the mint value of the gold coins would become greater than their market value as gold bullion, and such a divergence, in the case of a metal as valuable as gold, might easily lead to illicit coining on an extensive scale. To avoid this difficulty it would be necessary for the State to monopolize the extraction of gold. And this solution would have the additional merit of turning into more useful channels the labour and enterprise now employed in the not only useless but actually harmful activity of producing gold which is not wanted. Excessive production of gold would thus be guarded against. We should still, however, be liable to a fall of prices occasioned by the exhaustion of the gold supply.

APPENDIXES

APPENDIX A

SEIGNIORAGE AND PRICES

It is necessary to distinguish between an " open " mint and a " free " mint. A mint is said to be " open " to gold or silver when the State undertakes to coin *any quantity* of gold or of silver which is presented for coinage. Mintage is said to be " free " or " gratuitous " when no charge is made for mintage. A charge for coinage may be made either to cover the expenses of minting only, in which case the charge is termed *brassage*, or it may be levied at a higher rate so as to bring in a profit to the State, in which case it is termed *seigniorage*. It has become the custom, however, to use the term seigniorage loosely so as to include both kinds of charge.

The question—How does the imposition of seigniorage affect the level of prices ?—has some theoretical interest. In most cases the charge for seigniorage is small, but, for the sake of clearness, let us assume a charge of 50 *per cent.* of the value

of gold brought to be minted. Then, if one ounce
of gold is brought to the mint, half an ounce will be
returned to the bringer in the form of coin, and the
other half-ounce will be kept by the Government.
In this case the price of an ounce of gold bullion
cannot be appreciably less than half an ounce of
gold coin.   This relation is inevitable, for, if at any
time the price of an ounce of bullion *were* less than
half an ounce of coin, it would be profitable to take
bullion to the mint and get it transformed into coin
until the price of gold bullion rose to be half an
ounce of gold coin.   On the other hand, the price
of bullion may *rise above* the amount of half an
ounce of gold coin, and may continue to rise until
it amounts to a whole ounce of gold coin.   Above
that level it cannot rise, for were it to do so, it
would obviously be cheaper to melt down coin
than to buy bullion.   Let us suppose, then, that
this charge of 50 *per cent.* seigniorage is made in
an isolated country, in which the medium of circulation is gold coin, and in which the supply of
gold, produced from its own mines, is used either
for making money or for making ornaments.   Of
all gold brought to the mint one-half will be returned to the bringer in the form of coin, whilst
the other half is kept by the Government.   Now
what will be done with this other half-ounce ?   The
Government might sell it to bullion dealers, but

as, *ex hypothesi*, only such an amount of gold is
brought to the mint as is not required for the arts,
the gold so sold will merely cause an equal quantity
of gold, which would otherwise have been bought
by the same dealers, to go to the mint. It would
be simpler for the Government to coin their own
half-ounce immediately, instead of selling it in
exchange for coin. In either case the quantity of
gold coined will be the same ; it will be the total
quantity brought to the mint *including the amount
deducted as seigniorage.* Had there been no
seigniorage, other things being the same, the same
quantity of gold would have been brought to the
mint, but it would have been coined into pieces of
double the weight ; the number of coins issued,
and therefore the level of prices, would have been
one-half of what they are when a seigniorage of
50 *per cent.* is levied. In other words, the imposition of a seigniorage of 50 *per cent.*, if the
nominal value of the coins remains unaltered, will
mean a doubling of the price level.

In Chapter IV. it was shown that, in a country
with an open mint and gratuitous coinage, the price
of gold ornaments, as measured in gold coin, cannot
vary ; that an increase in the amount of coin, which
causes a rise in all other prices, will therefore not
affect the price of gold ornaments, and that such
an increase will therefore cause gold ornaments to

seem relatively cheap, and will lead to an increased demand for gold in the arts. But an increased demand for gold in the arts will lead to a decrease in the supply of gold brought to the mints, and this will tend to reduce the amount of coin, and hence the level of prices, to the former level. This process, it is important to notice, will not come into play where seigniorage is charged until prices have risen by the amount of the charge, *e.g.* by 10 *per cent.* if the seigniorage is 10 *per cent.* We have already shown that where seigniorage is levied, the price of bullion may vary between certain limits. Within these limits an increase in the quantity of money in circulation will cause the price of gold ornaments to rise in just the same way as the prices of all other commodities. Thus there will be no increased demand for gold for the arts, and consequently no check to the supply of gold for coinage, and no check to the rise of prices consequent upon additions to the coinage, until the level of prices has risen to correspond with the seigniorage. We thus reach the conclusion that, in an isolated country with an open mint, and a currency of gold only, the imposition of a seigniorage of 10 *per cent.* will, other things being equal, cause an increase of 10 *per cent.* in the volume of currency. It should be carefully noticed, however, that this argument applies only to an isolated country, and under the conditions described. Ricardo's reasoning, in his *Reply to Bosanquet*, that seigniorage has no effect upon prices is valid only upon the assumption that the metal taken by the State to satisfy its charges is not added to the circulation, and that there is a strict limitation of mintage. In this connection the reader may refer to the discussion of token money contained in Chapter II.

APPENDIX B

PROPORTION OF TOTAL MEDIA OF EXCHANGE TO CASH

Suppose an isolated country in which the total available stock of money-material, which we may call " gold," is 18,000 units. This will be partly in circulation and partly in the reserves of banks. If M represent the portion of this money in circulation, and V be its velocity, the total cash transactions of the country may be represented by MV. Similarly M′V′ will represent the total cheque transactions, where M′ is the amount of current deposits, and V′ the velocity of circulation of cheques. Let V be 25, and V′ 50. Further, suppose that the bankers keep a proportion of reserve to current accounts of 1 to 4. If, then, the amount of gold in banker's reserves be G, we have

$$M + G = 18,000 \quad . \quad . \quad . \quad (1)$$

First, let us suppose that the ratio of cash to cheque transactions is a steady one, say of 1 to 10. Then,

$$M'V' = 10 MV,$$

but $V' = 50$ and $V = 25$,

therefore $$M' = 5 M \quad . \quad . \quad . \quad . \quad (2)$$

Further, we have supposed that the total of current accounts is equal to four times the gold kept in reserve,

$$M' = 4 G \quad . \quad . \quad . \quad . \quad (3)$$

From equations (1), (2) and (3) it emerges that,

$$M = 8,000 \qquad G = 10,000$$
$$MV = 200,000 \qquad M' = 40,000$$
$$M'V' = 2,000,000$$

Therefore the ratio of gold currency, *plus* deposit currency to the total amount of gold in use, is

$$\frac{M+M'}{M+G} = \frac{48}{18}.$$

Still supposing that $M'V' = 10 MV$ let us assume the bankers to increase their loans to ten times, instead of four times, the amount of their gold reserves. We shall then have a similar series of equations, from which we get,

$$M = 12,000 \qquad G = 6,000$$
$$MV = 300,000 \qquad M' = 60,000$$
$$M'V' = 3,000,000.$$

Hence the ratio $\dfrac{M+M'}{M+G}=\dfrac{72}{18}$.

But if we assume no bond to exist between the quantities MV and M'V', *i.e.* if we assume that the amount of cheque transactions may increase without reference to the amount of cash transactions, we might (upon the above assumption that bankers increase the ratio of loans to reserve to 10 to 1) get the following figures,

$$M=8,000 \qquad\qquad G=10,000$$
$$MV=200,000 \qquad\qquad M'=100,000$$
$$M'V'=5,000,000,$$

in which case the ratio

$$\frac{M+M'}{M+G}=\frac{108}{18}.$$

Thus we see that a change in banking habits which, if the bond between MV and M'V' holds good, will cause the fraction $\dfrac{M+M'}{M+G}$ to alter in the ratio of 6 to 4, might, if the bond between MV and M'V' did not hold good, cause this fraction to alter in the ratio of 9 to 4. On the other hand, the fact that bankers keep a constant ratio between current accounts and reserve will have a very slight influence in keeping constant the fraction $\dfrac{M+M'}{M+G}$ if once the bond between MV and M'V' is broken.

APPENDIX C

Let us suppose the whole population of a country to be divided up into three groups : (1) commercial; (2) professional ; (3) wage-earners ; and let us assume that all members of classes (1) and (2) keep banking accounts, and that no member of class (3) keeps such accounts except in savings banks. Between these three classes, represented by the circles C, P, and W, there are flows of cash against goods, as shown on the diagram. It must be remembered in studying this diagram that we are dealing with cash, and cash only ; cheque transactions must be disregarded altogether. We see, then, that the professional class pays wages to W, and cash in purchase of goods to C ; the wage-earners pay rents and fees to P, and cash in purchase of goods to C ; the commercial men pay wages to W, and rents and fees to P.

Let us then take a typical member of each class and study the stream of cash which flows through his purse. As typical of the commercial class we will take a shopkeeper, C ; as typical of the pro-

[1] This analysis I have taken the liberty of modifying in the cause of simplicity.

fessional class, a doctor, P ; and as typical of the wage-earning class, a labourer, W. First, then, as to the cash receipts and outgoings of the shop-keeper, C. His cash receipts will come from three sources : (1) from the bank when he cashes cheques ; (2) from P, in exchange for goods purchased by P ; (3) from W, in exchange for goods purchased by W.

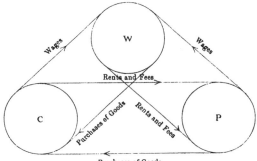
Purchases of Goods

These receipts we will denote by BC, PC, and WC respectively. Many large shops, and some small ones, pay their receipts into a bank daily, so that the cash received from P and from W is banked almost immediately, and is not available for further expenditure by C. We may suppose, however, that the typical shopkeeper, C, banks a part only of his cash receipts and uses another part, denoted by c, for expenditure on wages, etc., direct from

I

his till. Then the total cash available for expenditure by C will be BC+c, *i.e.* the money drawn out of his bank *plus* the money spent out of cash receipts. The cash expenditure of C will be the wages paid to W and the fees and rents paid to P ; quantities which may be represented by CW and CP respectively. It is reasonable to suppose that C's holding of cash in his till and purse remain constant. Assuming this, we have,

$$BC+c=CW+CP \quad . \quad . \quad . \quad (1)$$

Second, as to the cash receipts and expenditure of P. His receipts of cash consist of (1) money obtained by cashing cheques, (2) rents and fees paid by C, and (3) rents and fees paid by W, and may be represented by BP+CP+WP. The item BP will obviously be used for expenditure, as P will not cash a cheque unless he wants money to spend. The items CP and WP, on the other hand, may be dealt with in two ways. P may either pay them into his bank or use them to meet current expenditure. It is probable that he would do both, and also that he would use rather a larger proportion of these receipts for current expenditure than would a member of the commercial class. Whatever may be the sum thus used, however, let it be represented by p. Then the total amount of cash available for expenditure by P will be BP+p, *i.e.*

all money drawn by P from his bank *plus* the amounts paid out of other cash receipts. Turning next to P's cash expenditure, we see from the diagram that this will consist of the money paid to C in exchange for goods, together with the wages paid to W, and may be represented by PC+PW. Again assuming equality of cash income and expenditure, *i.e.* that P pays out just as much cash as he receives, less all amounts banked by him, we have,

$$BP + p = PW + PC \qquad . \qquad . \qquad . \quad (2)$$

Finally, as to the cash receipts and expenditure of W. His receipts may be assumed to consist entirely of wages paid to him by C or P, together with any money drawn by W from his savings bank, and may be represented by CW+PW+BW. His expenditure of cash, on the other hand, consists of rents and fees paid to P, and money paid to C in exchange for goods, together with any cash paid by W into his savings bank, and may be represented by WC+WP+WB. Equating these two expressions, we get,

$$CW + PW + BW = WC + WP + WB \qquad . \quad (3)$$

or,

$$WC + WP = CW + PW - (WB - BW)$$
$$= \text{wages received, less net deposits in savings bank.}$$

Adding together equations (1), (2) and (3) we get
$$PW+CW+PC+CP+WC+WP=BP+BC+p+c+$$
total wages paid—net deposits of wage-earners in
savings banks   .   .   .   .   .   (4)

But the left-hand side of this equation represents
the totality of transfers of cash against goods (including services) between C, P, and W, whilst
$BP+BC$ represents the total cash withdrawals of
P and C from their banks. If, then, we regard C,
P, and W as representing not individual members
of each class, but as the classes themselves, the left-
hand side of equation (4) comes to represent the
total transfers of cash against goods occurring
between these three classes of the community,
whilst $BP+BC$ will represent the cash withdrawn
from their banks by the professional and commercial classes—that is to say, by the whole banking
community. We may say, therefore, that the sum
total of transfers of cash against goods between
these three classes during any given period of time
is equal to :—

   (1) total withdrawals of cash from banks other
        than savings banks,
+(2) total wages paid,
+(3) total cash payments made from current re-
        ceipts by professional men,

+(4) total cash payments made from current receipts by commercial men,

−(5) net deposits of wage-earners in savings banks.

Now the total transfers of cash against goods here described is equivalent to the total of such transfers for the whole community, except that it leaves out the transfers of cash against goods *within each class*. But a little reflection will show that the *cash* transfers occurring between members of the working class are comparatively small in amount, whilst, practically speaking, all monetary transactions between different members of the professional or commercial classes are conducted through the medium of cheques. The omission, therefore, of transfers of cash against goods within each class is a matter of small importance. Also it will generally be admitted that terms (3), (4) and (5) of our last equation must be fairly small as compared with terms (1) and (2). It is, therefore, not far from the truth to say that the total transfers of cash against goods (including services) occurring within a given period *in the whole community* will be equal to the total withdrawals of cash from banks, other than savings banks, *plus* the amount of wages paid, during that period.

APPENDIX D

VELOCITY OF CIRCULATION OF DEPOSIT CURRENCY IN ENGLAND

It is unfortunate that, owing to the non-existence of the necessary material, we are not able to evaluate the velocity of circulation of metallic money in England. It is possible, however, even with the small amount of information at present available, to make a fairly accurate guess at the velocity of deposit currency. To evaluate this quantity we have to find out (1) the average total of current accounts during any year, and (2) the total value of the cheques drawn during that year. Neither of these quantities, however, is directly ascertainable. As regards current accounts, the banks, whilst showing the total amount of deposits, do not differentiate between deposit and current accounts. As regards cheques drawn, the clearing-house figures show cheques drawn by customers of one bank upon customers of other banks. They do not include cheques drawn upon each other by customers of the same bank. To obtain the total of current accounts for 1911, I have taken, with certain reservations, the total of " deposits " for all banks, as published in the *Banker's Magazine*, and divided by two. This gives the respectable figure of £474,000,000. To obtain the total of cheques drawn by customers of the same bank upon each other, the following expedient may be used. Let us suppose that Banks A, B, C, D . . . have current accounts to the amount of a, b, c, d . . ., so that the total of current accounts for the whole country is $a+b+c+d+$ . . . Then, assuming that the average velocity of deposit currency in any year is V, the total value of cheques drawn upon Banks A, B, C . . . will be aV, bV, cV . . . , whilst the total value of cheques drawn over the whole country will be $(a+b+c$ . . .$)$V. But if the total of cheques drawn upon Bank A during the year be aV, the total of cheques drawn by customers of Bank A upon other customers of Bank A will tend to be equal to $\dfrac{a}{a+b+c+ \ . \ . \ .}a$V, or to $\dfrac{a^2}{a+b+c+ \ . \ . \ .}$V. Therefore the total value of cheques drawn by customers of one bank upon other customers of the same bank will be for the whole country $\dfrac{a^2+b^2+c^2+ \ \cdot \ \cdot \ \cdot}{a+b+c+ \ . \ . \ .}$ V. This fraction works out to 20,600,000 V. Taking the total clearing-house figures for 1911 as £15,387,000,000, we get, for the total value of cheques drawn during 1911, the expression £15,387,000,000 + £20,600,000 V. Equating this expression to £474,000,000 V we get approximately

$$V = 34$$

It may be noted incidentally that according to this calculation the total value of cheques drawn upon the customers of the same bank by each other during 1911 was £690,400,000, whilst the total cheque transactions amounted to £16,077,400,000.

INDEX

137

www.ingramcontent.com/pod-product-compliance
Ingram Content Group UK Ltd.
Pitfield, Milton Keynes, MK11 3LW, UK
UKHW042146280225
455719UK00001B/133